WHEN WE WERE
BOUNCERS 2

D0920040

Paul Lazenby

PUNCH INNA FACE PUBLICATIONS
A division of 667765 BC Ltd.
Vancouver, Canada

PUNCH INNA FACE PUBLICATIONS
A division of 667765 BC Ltd.

208–179 Davie St.

Vancouver, BC, Canada V6Z 2Y1

Covers by Dacosta! at Chocolate Soop

ISBN 978-0-9938218-2-0

Available through Amazon.com, WhenWeWereBouncers.com, or your local bookseller.

TRIGGER WARNING

This book contains extreme violence, vulgar language,
and inappropriate behavior. If you feel that these things
are likely to disturb or offend you, then you are strongly advised
to put this book down and back away slowly.

DISCLAIMER

Selected names, places and details have been altered
in order to prevent storytellers from becoming
incarcerated, divorced, and/or prematurely deceased.

In Memory of
KEVIN "THE MONSTER" RANDLEMAN
KIMBO SLICE

TABLE OF CONTENTS

Monsters at the Door
Busted

FOREWORD

I met Paul Lazenby around 2008 in Vancouver, BC, while filming the major motion picture *Damage*. To this day I still cannot believe that movie did not win an Oscar for Best Picture, and it would be the second time I was overlooked for Best Actor after *The Condemned* in 2007. Sometimes it's tough to be an award-winning actor who has never won a goddamn award... but I digress. Back to Paul.

Paul and I have a lot in common, so we hit it off immediately and have been friends ever since. Between takes all we did was shoot the shit and exchange stories, and I found out that Paul has an extensive background in MMA, pro wrestling, stunts, bouncing, powerlifting, and other things that I will not detail in this foreword.

Now, everybody loves a good bar fight story — especially me — and I mention Paul's diverse background so you know that when he's talking about that kind of stuff, he has been there, done that, and knows what the hell he is talking about.

In pursuing his passions in life, Paul has met some incredibly talented and driven individuals who are wonderful human beings. That being said, he has also met, worked with, and hung out with some of the most outlandish, over the top, don't-give-a-shit-about-nothing, crazy motherfuckers walking God's green earth.

And that's who you're gonna find in his books.

The first *When We Were Bouncers* had me in stitches. The book moves quickly from story to story and person to person, and almost every page was dog-eared to mark my favorite stories. My attention span makes it hard for me to read most books, but I flew through all 270 pages like a speed-reader on amphetamines, laughing my ass off and shaking my head. Paul's immense storytelling skills helped him capture all the calamity, brutality and absurdity of every firsthand account, and I know that *When We Were Bouncers 2* will be more of the same.

When We Were Bouncers was only the third book I've read in close to ten years, and the book you're holding now is gonna make it four.

Thanks, Paul.

"Stone Cold" Steve Austin

316 Gimmick St.

Los Angeles, CA

2016

🐦 *@steveaustinBSR*

📷 *@steveaustinBSR*

🌐 *brokenskullranch.com*

*Austin (left) with the author on
the set of THE PACKAGE (2013)*

Chapter One

"THE WORLD'S MOST DANGEROUS MAN" KEN SHAMROCK

Photo courtesy Bas Rutten

"He went facedown in a big ol' puddle of blood, and I said, 'Oh my goodness, I just killed this dude!'"

There is no more important name in the world of mixed martial arts than that of pro wrestler, toughman boxer, bare-knuckle street fighter, founder/leader of the Lion's Den fight team, and UFC Hall-of-Famer Ken Shamrock.

Shamrock's appearance in the first-ever Ultimate Fighting Championship kicked off a rivalry with fellow legend Royce Gracie that both ignited and fed MMA's wildfire popularity throughout the 90s.

Less than a year later, Shamrock emerged victorious from a sixteen-man tournament to be crowned the inaugural champion of Japan's elite Pancrase Hybrid Wrestling organization.

Many wins in both UFC and Pancrase followed (including a defeat of Dan "The Beast" Severn that earned Shamrock the first UFC Superfight Championship), until Shamrock shifted his focus to the World Wrestling Federation in 1997.

A successful three-year run in pro wrestling was followed by a return to mixed martial arts, and over the following 16 years Shamrock would battle in various organizations including Pride Fighting Championships, UFC, and Bellator MMA.

Should someone ever decide to carve an MMA Mount Rushmore, it is a lead-pipe cinch that the face of "The World's Most Dangerous Man" will be one of those that adorn it.

Getting Started

I started out doing personal protection work and bouncing while I was in college. It was a great time for me because I could pretty much choose my own hours, especially with bosses who would work with me because I was playing football. I was able to play football [during the day] and then work at night, [so] I was able to make money and not put too much stress on my body other than when there was altercations. I enjoyed it, and I was good at it. I was really able to talk to people, and most of the time I was able to talk situations down.

Shamrock displays the spoils of victory in the Pancrase ring (Photo courtesy Susumu Nagao)

I had a really good knack for being able to stop things before they happened.

Still, I did have guns and knives pulled on me many times. But you know what? When [people] do that, I knew that they're probably not gonna use it. Most of the time, these guys were all posers and they just wanna pull it out to see everybody scream and hit the floor. A knife, well, that's more like they may use it. But a gun, most of the time when somebody brings something like that into a club, they just wanna make a statement.

When I was ten years old, before I went into the system and became a ward of the court, I got into a gang fight outside a 7-11 and got stabbed, had a blade stuck in my arm. [Because] I've been stabbed before, and I've had guns shoved in my face many, many times, [I know that] you'd have to be in a real different type of situation for someone to use it when they pull a weapon, especially if you're in a crowd. Most people are not gonna stand in the middle of a crowd, pull a weapon out and say, "Hey, look at me!" [if they intend to use it] So, any time anybody did pull a knife or gun on me, my first instinct was to attack them immediately and don't give them time to think. And the whole time I was bouncing, I never got shot, never got stabbed.

A Premiere Beating

Back around 1987 I started bouncing at The Premiere Club, the hottest club in Reno [Nevada]. It was a real upper-class type of club where [the bouncers] wore tuxedos and cummerbunds. I eventually became the head doorman, but this story happened when I had just started. I was working with a guy named Ken D'Amico.

I believe it was a Wednesday night, I was on the door and Ken was workin' the floor. I heard some screamin' going on, and I looked in the door and down the hallway and there was this big dude standing there with his two buddies behind him. The guy was probably about six-five or six-six, maybe 270 pounds, and [I'd find out later that] he played for Brigham Young University as a tight end. He was mouthing off with a smaller dude [who was] maybe six-one and 190 pounds, and they were going back and forth until the bigger dude grabbed the smaller one by the neck.

I ran in there and grabbed the big dude, spun him around and said, "Whoa, take it easy! What's going on?" I told the smaller guy, "Hey, get to hoppin'. Go to the [main] bar, get a drink, it's on me." Then I told the big dude I'd take him to the upper bar and get him a free drink as well, but when I motioned [toward the bar], he slapped my hand out of the way.

I looked at him and said, "Well, now you're gonna have to leave." At the time I was only about 205 pounds so he just looked at me and used some choice words, said he was gonna rip my head [off] and crap down my neck. So I said, "You've got one real choice here, because the other choice you're not gonna like. The first choice is to walk out of here on your own. Second choice is I'm gonna drag you out by your head."

He laughed, and then he went to swing at me. But even though this was well before [I fought in] UFC, I had wrestled freestyle a whole lot in high school and after, so I was able to get around behind him and grab him in a rear neck crank. I kicked his feet out so I could bring him down and have him leaning back into me, and then I drug him out the door.

I was pulling him out backwards with my arm across his throat and his head stuck in my chest, and his two buddies started following me out. But they didn't touch me as I slammed both doors open, got the guy through the door, and let go of him. Well, I guess he had passed out from me choking him, and [when I let go] he dropped right down to the ground. His two buddies stopped, looked, and then one of 'em darted toward the parking lot. The other one started mouthin' off to me, so I put my back to the wall just as Ken [D'Amico] arrived outside and a crowd started to gather.

The dude on the ground [came to and] stood up, and then these other two guys I hadn't seen before ran out of the club and grabbed him, pushed him up against the wall and started tellin' him, "Dude, chill out!" I guess they must have been friends of his, he must have been going in there to meet them. But friends or not, he ended up punching one of 'em, shoving the other one out of the way, and then he ran towards me. And this is when everything slowed down for me.

It was like I was watching this big ol' horse run at me, and as he threw his punch I rolled under it, came up with a right hand, and hit him in the chin — *BOOM!* Stopped him dead motion, right in his tracks. I remember seeing blood just splat on the wall behind him as his head spun around. He went facedown and blood went right around his head, a big ol' puddle of blood, and I said, "Oh my goodness, I just killed this dude." Everybody started screamin', girls started cryin', and the ambulance came and picked him up. But the guy never woke up — he actually went into a coma and we had to go to court.

MAULER'S NOTE: As detailed in Shamrock and Richard Hanner's book INSIDE THE LION'S DEN, Shamrock's assailant eventually came out of the coma after emergency surgery was performed to remove a grapefruit-sized blood clot from his head.

When the trial came, [International Boxing Hall of Fame member] Mills Lane was the judge! (laughs) He ruled that it was "mutual combat", which meant that we were both at fault, so nobody was at fault. But then [the guy I punched] took it to civil court, and that didn't go so well. You see, the dude's dad was the game warden, so you could imagine the troubles I had trying to find an attorney to defend me! (laughs)

The club got shut down [because of the incident]. You can look that up, it was a big story in Reno. Even today, people still talk about it.

@ShamrockKen

@ShamrockKen

www.KenShamrock.com

Chapter Two

CHRIS "FACHE" BRUNO

Photo courtesy Chris Bruno.

"All I hear is 'rippelly-rip, crackelly-crack' as this guy shreds my shirt and punches me in the head over and over."

Surfer, skier, baseball player, fighter — Connecticut native Chris "Fache" Bruno brings an impressive list of real-world credentials to his decades-long career in acting.

After making his name on the soap operas *All My Children* and *Another World*, Bruno amassed a plethora of impressive career credits including a role alongside Sir Anthony Hopkins in *The World's Fastest Indian*.

While in Vancouver, Canada playing Sheriff Walt Bannerman on the TV series *The Dead Zone*, Bruno joined the FKP MMA fight team and battled in a number of mixed martial arts and submission grappling tournaments. Recent years have seen him appear on *Prison Break, Castle, NCIS: Los Angeles*, and *The Fosters*, as well as co-writing, co-producing, and starring in the feature film *A Remarkable Life*.

As if all that weren't enough, Bruno also speaks fluent French, used to date Debbie Gibson, is the godfather to Kelly Ripa and Mark Consuelos' oldest son, owns one of the most intimidating (and friendliest) dogs in the world, and can fart on command at whatever pitch, volume and length he chooses.

Buying In

I wasn't just a bouncer, I was also a bar owner. I used to own a bar called Vermouth on [New York's] upper west side. But I definitely did a bouncer's job too, because I had to "regulate" from time to time. (laughs)

I had actually started at that place as a bartender five years before, but I got fired two weeks before Christmas. The owners were like, "Chris, you're a great guy but you're too focused on the acting business. That's as it should be because you're probably gonna do great, but we need a career bartender." They told me I was welcome to come in with my friends and drink for free anytime, but I was still like, "Fuck ME!" (laughs) But then *Another World* happened so it was all good, and I always stayed on good terms with the guys who fired me.

Five years later, it was the mid-90s — I was on *All My Children* at the time — and Danny, one of the club's owners, approached me and said that he was thinking about expanding. He wanted to make his place into a restaurant/nightclub where they would put the tables away at around eleven and keep it going till late. He asked me if I wanted to buy in, and it looked good to me. So I ended up going into business with the same guys who fired me five years before! (laughs)

World Series Throwdown

This story happens on the night that the Yankees won the World Series, I think it was in 1996. When Wade Boggs was riding around the stadium on the back of a police horse and shit. My boys from [my hometown in] Connecticut had come to town in a big limo, and they told me, "Yeah, we're coming to your fuckin' club after the game, we'll hang out!" The whole city was insane that night, traffic was at a standstill and people were partying in the streets, but somehow my friends made it to the bar and we had a great time.

Our doorman that night was a guy named Larry Doby Jr. Larry's father was a real history-maker — he was the first African-American to play in the ABL [precursor to the NBA], the second one to be signed to a major league [baseball] team, the first one to play in the American League, and the first one to go directly from the Negro Leagues to the majors. Larry Sr. was also one of the first two black players to win a World Series, the first black home run league leader, and the first black player to hit a World Series home run.

Larry Jr. used to play, too — I think he played on the [Chicago] White Sox' farm team for a while. He was a monster, just a badass. Maybe six-four, and 235 or 240. He used to come play with us out in Long Island, and the first time [he came out] he said, "Yeah, I haven't played in a while" and then hit two fuckin' BOMBS right up onto the Grand Central Parkway! (laughs) In both of his first two at-bats, he just CRUSHED these four-hundred-foot shots, man!

So anyway, Larry's on the door that night, and at one point my buddy Georgie gets up and walks across the bar. Then, out of the corner of my eye, I see this dude just punching Georgie in the face! What the fuck?! So I go and grab the dude, start taking him out, and then Larry appears and grabs Georgie. But I tell Larry that Georgie's with me and that I got the other guy, so it's all cool as I walk Georgie's attacker to the door.

Or so I think.

Now, the UFC was still pretty new at the time, and I had just seen my first UFC fight and realized, "I'm a street fighter and I can scrap, but these guys can REALLY fight. I gotta learn to fight like this." So I'd gone to my very first Muay Thai class that same day and learned how to Thai kick, which was about to come in very handy. (laughs)

I get this guy out the door, and I'm thinkin' he's just gonna walk away. But suddenly he slams on the brakes and back-elbows me right in the fuckin' forehead! I immediately crack him with an overhand right, then I grab his shirt and feed him with an uppercut and he goes out. But as he's dropping, a buddy of his who I didn't know about jumps on my back and tackles me into a parked car. So now it's on with me and this guy! The car alarm's goin' off, and remember that World Series celebrations are happening so people all around us are climbing lampposts and jumping up and down on parked cars and running riot, and it's just fucking INSANE.

I get to my feet and manage to get this dude off my back, and as I square up with him, my first instinct is to kick that mother-fucker in his leg just as hard as I can. So I fuckin' NAIL him in his front leg with a roundhouse [kick] that I just learned, and I land it so hard that it sweeps him, takes him right off his feet! Then I feed him with another fuckin' shot and jump on him, and all I hear is *rippelly-rip, crackelly-crack* as this dude shreds my shirt and punches me in the head over and over. By now the club is emptying out, and his friends and mine all swarming into the street. Everybody's goin' at it and I'm just smokin' dudes in the face.

We finally get these guys subdued and loaded into a cab, and by now my shirt's ripped right down the front, I'm basic-ally standing there shirtless. As the cab pulls away, my partners look at me and go, "What the FUCK, Bruno? You're usually, like, the mellowest guy! We've never seen violence like that before!" (laughs) I guess a little switch got flipped when I got hit with that elbow.

The next day, I go back and tell my Muay Thai coach — who I just started training with, remember — I tell him, "Last night I got in a scrap and I kicked this guy with a roundhouse, took his legs right out." He just looks at me for a minute and goes, "*What the fuck?!* I've never had a dude come in here and learn something, then instantly use that shit in the street the same day! What is *wrong* with you, man?" (laughs)

The worst part of this story is that earlier that night my mom was in the bar, and while she was there we caught some guy in the bathroom, stashing a chick's purse that he'd stolen. I had dragged the guy outside and he shoved me, which is a real trigger for me. When somebody shoves me, nine times out of ten I'm gonna swing on the guy. But I knew that my mom was watching through the front window, and I was like, "I am NOT gonna scrap in front of my mother." (laughs) So I just told my partner Danny to call the cops, and I held the guy until they arrived and arrested him.

As my mom was leaving that night, she said, "I'm so proud of you, Chris. I'm surprised you didn't just paste the guy in his face. He deserved it, but you didn't do it. I'm really happy and proud, you're really growing up."

So of course she brings it up again the next day, and I gotta tell her, "Um... actually, after you left I wasted two dudes right in front of the bar!" (laughs)

🐦 *@chrisbruno16*
📷 *@thefachelife*

Chapter Three

FRANKIE KAZARIAN

All photos courtesy Frankie Kazarian.

"It was like one of those Popeye brawls, where it's just a huge puff of smoke with arms and legs sticking out everywhere."

Since breaking into the pro wrestling business in 1998, Frank Gerdelman aka Frankie Kazarian has established himself as one of the industry's most established and respected workers.

His career highlights are too numerous to include in their entirety, but of particular note are his pedigree as a student of all-time great Killer Kowalski, his multiple TNA/Impact Wrestling tag team and X-division championships, and his reigns as the inaugural champion/first-ever two-time champion of the cult favorite Pro Wrestling Guerilla promotion.

At the time of this writing he is also a two-time Ring of Honor (ROH) world tag team champion with "The Fallen Angel" Christopher Daniels, a team for which Kazarian's band VexTemper provides the official theme music.

Hitting the Ground Running

Around late '98 or early '99, I finished my training [in professional wrestling] with Killer Kowalski and moved from Massachusetts back to California. I was working at my friend's gym and my parents' tanning salon, but I decided to take another job at night as a bouncer for a little extra money to support my wrestling habit.

[The bouncing job] was in Palm Springs, California at a place called Zelda's Nightclub — which wasn't nearly as much fun as the video game, trust me. It was probably the biggest nightclub in Palm Springs at the time, and it had two sections — the smaller section would be open on Wednesdays and Thursdays, and then on Friday-Saturday they had both sides open.

I learned very early on that the other "door hosts" — we weren't allowed to call ourselves bouncers — were just there to do blow, get drunk and get laid. I was probably the only one taking the gig seriously! I had just turned twenty-one, and I was so tunnel-visioned on wrestling that I was legitimately just there to my job. Stupid me. (laughs) I'm not a club person anyway, I'm more of a dive bar guy, but back then it was especially new to me.

On my first night it's pretty mellow, until all of a sudden I hear this scuttlebutt in the back. I go running over there and I immediately see one of our cocktail waitresses bleeding from the head, just pouring blood! One of the bouncers is struggling with this guy, so I go over to help and try to assess the situation. I eventually find out that she got attacked because she had been thwarting the guy's advances. He was punching clock with her and she was having none of it, so of course what do you do in a situation like that except take a highball glass against the girl's head?

Her head's pouring blood, we have to rush her to the nearest hospital, and she's crying and screaming *"I'm a model! This is gonna ruin my career!"* Keep in mind this is Palm Springs, we're not in South Central or something. At worst I was expecting pull-aparts between old golfers or something, but instead we have a girl getting her face smashed with a glass within the first couple hours of my first shift!

Got a Light?

A few weeks later, I'm working near the front door and I see this drunk girl leaning over to talk to whatever dude was with her that night. Her hair is just filled with hair spray, and as she leans over, she's getting closer and closer to this candle that's sitting on the table. I'm sitting by the bar watching this and doing commentary with the bartender Jamie: "It's gonna happen... she's leaning in... almost there... AWWWW, she leaned back!" (laughs) This went on for about ten minutes until she finally leaned in too close and... *WHOOF!* The guy she's talking to is really quick though, and right away he puts it out with his napkin. But she's so hammered that she barely registers that anything happened, she's just sitting there with her head all steaming! (laughs) We told the guy, "Dude, you should have just let her catch fire, it would have been so much funnier!"

Frat Bastards

I'd been there about six months when a bunch of frat guys rolled in one night — big 'ol, corn-fed, white frat guys. Right away it's one of those situations where you go, "Shit, no good can come out of this." And sure enough, ten minutes later there's a giant fight. It was like one of those Popeye brawls, where it's just a huge puff of smoke with arms and legs sticking out everywhere.

We all carried flashlights so if any shit went down, you were supposed to shine your light so [the other bouncers] saw it. I'm in the middle of this melee and I'm shining my light, shining my light, shining my light... and then I get CLOCKED in the back of the head with still no help in sight! I'm in there for a good ten minutes overall, and there was not a single other bouncer to be seen!

Somehow I got out of there alive, and later I come to find out what happened to my backup — one guy was doing coke out in the parking lot, one guy was downstairs having intercourse, and two of the other guys were at the back bar and didn't see me. That's when it really hit me that I had to watch my back, because I had nobody in this place that I could depend on.

Mark the Shark

One night this guy gets into a fight — like, an actual punching fight — with a girl. For once my coworkers are on the ball and a couple of us grab him, a couple of us grab her, and we take them both outside. We've got them sat down on the curb so we can find out what happened, and during the conversation somebody must have mentioned that the cops were on their way because out of the corner of my eye I see the dude suddenly jump up and take off. I run after him and

Kazarian showin' off his half of the ROH world tag team
championship.

catch up with him, then waist-lock him and kind of belly-to-back
[suplex} him to the ground. Not dropping him onto the top of his
head or anything, just taking him down so I can hold him until the
other guys get there.

Then the other guys run over and... man, those guys used to take
liberties. One guy we called "Mark the Shark" immediately fish-
hooks the guy, just takes his thumbs and starts ripping [the guy's
mouth]. Another guy comes up from behind and smashes the guy's
ankle, and then everybody's just beating the shit out of the guy. At
that point I let go, because I've never been into beating guys up un-
necessarily. It's something that I never would do, so I back away and
the guy is just bleeding everywhere.

The cops finally show up — they were always really cool with us, by the way — and after they get the guy and take him away in handcuffs, one of them comes over to me and asks, "Were you involved in that?" I tell him yes, and then he sees blood on my shirt — we always wore tuxedo vests and long-sleeved white shirts — and he asks, "Is that his blood on you?" I say yes again, and then the cop gives me a funny look and says, "Well, uh, this guy is known to us and... I have to tell you that he has AIDS. Not HIV, full-blown AIDS."

Now I'm FURIOUS. I'm so mad because I was just trying to restrain the guy, I didn't want to bust him open like that. I checked right away, and luckily I had no open wounds and the blood was only on my vest and sleeves. But it still freaked me out, and it was a tense two or three months before I could be sure that I didn't have anything. It pissed me off so much, because [the other bouncers] didn't have to beat the guy up like that. What a rotten way that would have been to get such a terrible disease!

Jaw-Jacking Jarhead

Palm Springs is next to a Marine base, Twentynine Palms. We would sometimes see some of the younger Marines right out of boot camp that think they're invincible, you know? There was always a few that just have that attitude. One night a couple of 'em came in, and immediately I was like, "Shit, something's gonna happen."

Only five or ten minutes later, it did. One of our "door hosts" was off-duty and dancing with his girl when one of the Marines started talking to her. Then [the other Marine] came up behind my coworker and punched him right in the back of the head! I ran straight over and grabbed the Marine who did the punching, threw him in what I only knew at the time as a "Tazmission" (laughs), which of course is really a kata-hajime [judo choke].

Then I started dragging him backwards, and while I'm dragging him and squeezing his neck, the guy starts furiously tapping on my arm over and over. My manager Rod is close by, and he yells at me, "The guy's tapping! He's tapping!" and I go, "Rod, I don't give a fuck! I'm not looking to win a *match!*" (laughs) I drag the guy down two flights of stairs while giving him just enough air to stay awake, and then I shove him out the door. As soon as he's out there he starts screaming, "You're lucky, man! I woulda killed you!" and so on. By now I've had enough, so I'm just like, "Okay man, okay. You're right, I'm lucky. Good night."

That was the moment I finally decided that it was time to quit, and the next week I went in and gave my resignation. I left on good terms and everything, but I'd definitely had enough.

What I Got Out of It

Looking back, I have to say that [bouncing] was a really good learning experience. Especially finding out how... hmm, how do I say this without offending the female sex... how, well, *dumb* some women are. I couldn't believe how wearing that stupid Zelda's vest and shirt made you more attractive than the average Joe. How these dumb, stupid, drunken girls would behave around you, just because you were the bouncer. It's like, "Where is this coming from? I'm a guy making five bucks an hour at best, I can offer these girls nothing, but I'm attractive because I'm wearing this stupid vest." It showed me a lot about how the brain of the inebriated female clubber really works.

But starting out as a young guy without a whole lot of confidence, that job really helped me go from a boy to a man, I'll tell ya that. It was fun, I wouldn't trade it for anything, but I wouldn't necessarily go back and do it again! (laughs)

@FrankieKazarian

@VexTemper

@frankiekazarian_official

Chapter Four

ROB HAYTER

All photos courtesy Rob Hayter.

**"He looks me right in the eye and says,
'I'm going to come back and I'm going to kill you.
I mean it, and I want you to remember that.'"**

As an actor, stuntman, stunt/fight coordinator, capoeira instructor, jujutsu black belt, and all-around stand-up muthafucka, Rob Hayter brings a wealth of character, experience and ability to every production on which he works. If you've seen *Man of Steel*, *White House Down*, *Elysium*, *Fantastic Four*, or the hit TV show *Lucifer* (to name just a few), then you've definitely seen Rob's work.

Two of his most notable credits are the feature films *Deadpool* (in which he played the character "Hydra Bob") and *I Love You Beth Cooper* (for which he withstood a car hit of sufficient brutality to net him a World Stunt Award for "Hardest Hit").

He also once worked me so hard during a capoeira class that I nearly puked.

Dick.

Shambhala

One of the hairiest situations of my career happened while I was running the nighttime security crew at Shambhala, a giant, five-day electronic music festival that's held every summer near Nelson, British Columbia. It was about the midway point of the festival and I had just finished a thirteen-hour shift. The sun was up and blazing, and I was in my overheated tent trying to catch a few hours of sleep. I wasn't having much success because at Shambhala it doesn't matter what time it is, that doesn't mean shit. The party's perpetually on, and good luck trying to get some quiet time.

It didn't help that it was the first year they decided to have daytime helicopter tours of the festival. So all day long this chopper is taking off, buzzing the festival, and landing. Over and over again. Yeah, try sleeping through that. (laughs)

I'm lying there with my radio beside me because the security staff's on standby pretty much all of the time, and the call comes in that there's a crisis happening down at the beach. Some guy's going nuts and the on-duty security guys need a hand to restrain him. So I curse under — and over — my breath, drag my ass out of my tent, hop in one of the vans and bomb on down there.

When I get to the scene, I find out that the crazy guy is actually the new boyfriend of an acquaintance of mine, and he's also a new immigrant from Croatia. The guy's pretty much straight off the boat after living in an actual war zone, and he's got barely enough English to get by. Fantastic. As if that's not enough, the dude's FLYING on a cocktail of weed, hard liquor, and acid. Now, anybody who's sleep-deprived and on that mixture is gonna be a problem, but think about *this* guy for a second — a Croatian on acid, straight out of a war zone, and he's hearing HELICOPTERS. Not exactly "shiny, happy people holding hands!" (laughs)

There's four of us and we've got the truck, we've got our zap straps, and we're ready to go. Me and one other guy try to talk to the dude first, but we're wearing black fatigues and black shirts so all he sees is Serbian military coming to pull him out of his house. He's fully wigging out, taking wild swings at anyone who

L. Hayter doubling Sharlto Copley in ELYSIUM. R. Hayter displaying his world stunt award with longtime capoeira instructor Mestre Eclilson de Jesus

tries to help him, and I know that there's no way in hell this is gonna end well.

Finally, with no other option, two of us take the guy down and put our combined bodyweight on him, which would normally be the end of the scenario. But you may remember me saying that this guy's on acid and in genuine fear for his life, so no matter how hard we try to pin him, he just keeps lifting us off of him and screaming, *"THEY'RE TRYING TO KILL ME!!! THEY'RE TRYING TO KILL ME!!!"*

So the other two guys pile on, and we finally manage to get the zap straps on his wrists and get him packed into the truck. The whole time he's going absolutely insane, even with his wrists bound together it's all we can do to keep him under control. But finally we get him relatively secure, and with his girlfriend also on board, the truck starts rolling away.

We're driving for a minute or two when, as suddenly as if somebody flicked a switch, the guy completely stops screaming and fighting. We all catch our breath as he lays there facedown and motionless, and after a few more minutes go by I figure the storm has passed. Silly me. (laughs) Just as I start to relax a little, the guy slowly and calmly lifts his head off the truck bed, turns his face toward me, looks me right in the eye and says, "I'm going to come back here and I'm going to kill you. I mean it, and I want you to remember that."

Jesus Christ. (laughs)

We take him back to a chill-out tent that has soft couches and soothing music for people who are freaking out, and we wrap him in a blanket and get his girlfriend to stay with him. Thankfully, after an hour or so the drugs start wearing off, and he realizes that he's not in Croatia anymore and becomes a much more reasonable person.

It's a big relief for me when I watch his girlfriend finally drive him off the site, knowing that I won't have to spend the rest of the festival looking over my shoulder for a Croatian psychopath with PTSD. But then I realize that the festival's only half-over, which means sixty more hours of knock-outs, pass-outs, and drug-fueled wig-outs.

And people wonder why I laugh my ass off when they ask if I miss the excitement of running a security team! (laughs)

Trouble with the MC

A while later I was working at an after-hours party in a suburb of Vancouver called Burnaby, at a film and TV lighting warehouse. Most of the lighting gear had been moved off to the side and covered with tarps to make room for a bar, a raised DJ booth, and two massive floor spaces for dancing. It wasn't a licensed event so they didn't officially have liquor on the premises — but of course, they had liquor on the premises. (laughs)

At about 2:30 AM a guy showed up with a few cronies, and although he wasn't wearing any identifying clothing, my coworker Johnny recognized him as a high-ranking member of a well-known, um, "motorcycle enthusiast club." The party promoter also recognized the guy, and was immediately intimidated to the point of sucking up to the crew by buying them drinks.

Johnny didn't think that was a good idea and neither did I, especially when more bikers showed up with a few strippers in tow. They were followed by more and more until we had almost twenty of them in the place, all getting progressively drunker on the promoter's tab.

Needless to say, Johnny and I got pretty hyper-aware. By 3:30 the DJ had gone into high gear, everybody's "party favors" were kicking in, a certain white powder was in heavy use in the bathroom stalls, and the potential for something to kick off was at its peak. We knew that if something was gonna happen, it was probably going to happen soon.

I decided to do a walk-through to make sure that nobody was getting into too much trouble, and I strolled into the back where there was a long, narrow hallway flanked on either side by scaffolding and production gear. My heart sank as I came across a couple of strippers standing off to the side of two dudes who were squared off with each other. Their body language told me that they weren't setting up for a bro-hug.

I had just noticed that one of the guys was a fellow stunt performer, let's call him "Karl", when — *BAM!* — he NAILS the other guy with a solid punch right in the beak! It was a good shot — no talking, no posing, just WHAM. The other guy didn't even get his hand off the nearest stripper's ass before Karl was all over him with a series of right hands — *POP, POP, POP, POP, POP.* One of the strippers started screaming but Karl didn't stop, throwing his victim down between the scaffold beams and jackhammering away with more rapid-fire shots. Within seconds there was blood everywhere, and Karl had pushed the guy's nose right over to the side of his face.

I jumped in to break it up, but two heavies appeared out of nowhere to pull me away. That's when I got a good look at the dude on the bottom, and oh, shit — it was the head guy from the local chapter of the bike club!

Karl must have seen something in my expression, because he immediately got this horrified look on his face and started scampering deeper underneath the scaffolding. At that point, Johnny and a few other bouncers arrived, which kicked off a couple of minutes of our guys pushing and shoving and wrestling with theirs.

Karl eventually popped out the other side of the scaffolding, but since there were bikers everywhere he got grabbed almost immediately and pinned against the DJ booth. I got free of the shoving match and ran over to see Karl surrounded by a semicircle of thugs, all wearing three-quarter-length black leather coats and expressions that didn't give me much hope for Karl's future.

They threw him down and began stomping the bajeezus out of him, and through all of this the DJ just kept playing, completely oblivious to the fact that somebody might be dying right in front of him. I tried to work my way through the crush of bodies, but one of the bikers turned around, put a hand underneath his coat and said, "You don't want to get involved." Which at that point, I certainly didn't. (laughs)

The only saving grace was that Karl seemed to know what he was doing. He was curled into a tight ball with his back against the DJ booth, taking as many of the shots on his shins and forearms as he could. Meanwhile, those mooks were falling all over each other trying to get a solid kick in, and with no idea how to work as a team, they were kicking each other in the legs more than they were kicking Karl.

Still, things weren't looking good so Johnny ran around behind the DJ booth, crawled through the space underneath, and pulled Karl out the back. Karl didn't need to be told what to do next — he sprang up, ran out the door, sprinted across the parking lot, and climbed over a fence to get away.

An hour later I was standing at the front door when a convoy of four black sedans flanked by four Harleys pulled up. The blacked-out rear window of one of the cars rolled down, and the guy behind it called me over. He looked up and said, "The guy who was in that fight — is he here?" I shook my head. He stared me down for a few seconds, then said, "If you see him again, you let us know." I nodded, and they drove off. Thankfully, that was the last of it for the rest of the night.

Karl didn't show his face in town for at least a month, and eventually a meeting was set up between him and the "motorcycle enthusiasts" to sort the situation out. Surprisingly, Karl ended up getting a bye on the whole thing based on the fact that the guy he had pummeled wasn't wearing any club identification. Since Karl didn't know at the time who he was beating up, it was ruled that he hadn't disrespected the club.

While it worked out in the end, I'm glad Karl knew enough to initially get out of Dodge. I'm not exaggerating when I say that doing that probably saved his life.

@robhayter

@robhayter

www. robhayter.com

Chapter Five

JERRY "GOLDEN BOY" TRIMBLE

All photos courtesy Jerry Trimble.

"He has this dude in a headlock, and suddenly he starts yelling, 'JERRY, GET HIM! HE'S GOT MY NUTS!'"

Sixth-degree taekwondo black belt Jerry "Golden Boy" Trimble is a familiar name to anyone who followed the North American kickboxing/full contact karate scene during the 80s. One of the fastest and flashiest kickers in the sport (his hook kick was clocked at 118 MPH), the savagely-aggressive Trimble had his best year in 1986 when he won world titles in both the Professional Kickboxing Association (PKA) and the Professional Karate Council (PKC).

After retiring in 1990, Trimble moved to Hollywood to pursue an acting career. Since then he has starred in over forty television and feature film productions, with his career highlights including onscreen battles with Tom Cruise in *Mission: Impossible 3* and "Stone Cold" Steve Austin in *The Package*.

Currently, Trimble divides his time between Los Angeles, CA and Vancouver, Canada with his wife and fellow actor Ami Dolenz.

Savage Samoan at Sneakers

My first bouncing gig was in Los Angeles around '91 or '92, at a place called Sneakers in Redondo Beach. I was in good shape, about 165 pounds at the time, and I had retired [from professional fighting] but was getting ready to come out of retirement. I was training at [kickboxing legend Benny Urquidez'] Jet Center, and Benny wanted to put me on the American kickboxing team to fight in Thailand. I was all for it, but then movies started happening so I figured [the comeback] wasn't meant to be.

Jerry didn't earn dual world championships by being a nice freakin' guy.

Anyway, on my first night at Sneakers the manager came up to me and said, "I'll tell you what we're gonna do — we're gonna have you be the 'good-time guy'". Right away I was thinking, "What the fuck is a 'good-time guy?'" (laughs) He said, "It's a great role in our establishment — you're still gonna be a bouncer and back the other guys up, but you're also going to walk around with roses and candy and other gifts to give to the pretty ladies in the club." So I said, "Oh, okay," but in my head I'm thinking, "You've gotta be kidding me — I just wanna be a bouncer, this is ridiculous!"

But it actually ended up being pretty cool. I'd go up to ladies, and also couples, carrying a big basket of roses. I'd introduce myself, hand out roses, and make sure everybody was having, well, a good time. As far as my security duties were concerned, I also had to keep my ears open for a "Code Red" call which meant a fight in whatever section — this was a huge place so they had it divided into sections.

Sure enough I eventually hear, "Code Red, Section Nine" on my radio. But it's my first night so I'm looking around the room and counting off the sections, trying to figure out which one is Nine! (laughs) Then I hear [a commotion] on my left, so I put my flowers down and bolt over there where I see a big Samoan guy fighting with another one of the customers. He KOs the other customer, then knocks out one of our bouncers who came up to try and stop him.

Now, the staging of this club has different levels and I'm on a level that puts me higher than the Samoan guy, so I leap off of it and over some chairs to hit this guy right in the chest with a flying side kick. He goes flying back into a railing and falls to the ground, and then gets up with his back to me. So I leap on him and grab the rails on either side of him, trying to keep him pinned there, and now he's leaning back and trying to head-butt me while I'm hanging on and trying to subdue him by kneeing him in the side and in the ass.

Finally, the other bouncers show up and say, "Okay, let him go, we got him!" I ask 'em, "Are you sure?" and they say, "Yeah, let 'im go!" So I let go and run back a couple of steps, and then the Samoan guy goes CRAZY! He starts hittin' the bouncers and they've got NO CLUE how to handle the situation. I'm floating around the outside, looking for a spot to jump back in again as the [other] bouncers barely manage to drag him to another section of the club. A spot finally opens after he knocks one bouncer down and throws another one off, so I go

Jerry shows off the freakish flexibility that made him one of the most feared kickers in the game.

around behind him and wrap my arm around his neck. I wasn't choking him on purpose because I didn't know jiu-jitsu or any of that stuff back then, I was just grabbin' the guy and got lucky [that it ended up as a choke].

He smashes me back against a table but that just sinks the choke deeper, and then I jump up and wrap my legs around him, squeezing with everything I've got. He falls back on top of me — *BOOM!* — and it hurts, but after that I'm thinking, "Okay, now I've got 'im." The bouncers are all standing over me and I'm telling them, "Get the fucking cops, get the fucking cops!" because this is the second time I have this guy and I sure as hell don't want to let him go until the cops arrive. But once again they tell me, "No, let him go, this time we've got 'im!" I didn't want to do it, but they refused to call the cops until I finally said, "Okay," and let the guy go. Well, the Samoan gets back up and just starts fuckin' WAILING on the bouncers again! (laughs) I back up to watch and it's chaos, the guy's going nuts.

At that point, I see the manager waiting by the front door for the cops to come. So I go and get my flowers, walk over to the manager and say, "You know what? Here's your flowers — FUCK YOU. Your guys have no idea what they're doing. I quit!"

Thankfully, [my movie career] picked up shortly after that. I ended up doing an average of three gigs a year, so I didn't need to go back to that bullshit! (laughs)

Being the Problem

I bounced in a couple of other places, but I had kind of a name by then so there wasn't too much trouble. A buddy of mine owned a couple of nightclubs, so he'd hire me to come in and make a hundred bucks a night without having to do too much for it.

Jerry with the great Al Pacino

To be honest, most of my bar fights happened on my off time — sometimes after I'd already fought in the ring that night! It got so bad that I'd fight in one bar, get kicked out and suspended from going there, then go to another place and have the doorman say, "Jerry, what are you doing? You're barred from here until Saturday!" (laughs) I had a lot of anger back then, I was an angry kid, and I'd unleash that anger both in and out of the ring.

Present from Mom

I used to be the personal trainer and bodyguard for Glenn Hughes of Deep Purple and Black Sabbath — later on he also played with Jason Bonham in Black Country Communion. This was around '83 or '84, and my job was to protect Glenn not only from being assaulted, but also from people who were giving him drugs and shit. That was kind of hard to do because we were both partying most of the time, so it was like, "Oh, man — I'm not doing my job!" (laughs)

One night we were in Atlanta, at an after-hours place called Club 112. [The place] opens at eleven or twelve at night and goes on till around six in the morning. It's about 3 AM when I leave Glenn in a corner with some friends and go to the bathroom. While I'm in there, my keys fall out of my pocket and I bend over to pick 'em up. Then, for whatever reason, this guy walks in front of me and sticks his crotch right in my face! I stand up and say, "What the fuck is your problem? I drop my keys and you stick your dick in my face?!" But the guy just looks at me and says, "Fuck you!" The bouncers quickly hear that there's trouble in the bathroom, and when they see that it's me, they say, "Jerry, you wanna take him outside?" And of course I say, "Fuck, yeah!" Now, I always used to wear what I called a "Mr. T Starter Kit," [which was] a bunch of rings and gold chains and shit (laughs). One of those rings was given to me by my mom, and it was

Jerry goes kick-for-kick with the legendary Jet Li in THE MASTER (1992)

made of gold with the initials "JT" spelled out in diamonds. Every time I got into a fight, I would switch it to my first finger so it would cut [my opponent]. Like I said, I had a lot of anger, man.

So I switch the ring as we walk out behind the nightclub, and a big crowd of people follows us. The guy starts loosening up, juking with his arms and shit, and I can tell that he knows what he's doing, he knows how to box. We start bouncing around, feeling each other out, and suddenly the guy slips in with a really nice jab and gets me right in the mouth! So I skip inside and hit 'im right in the eye — *BOOM* — and then I start pummeling the hell out of 'im. When it's obvious that he's out, [the bouncers] pull me away and I go inside to get Glenn. But as we leave, I look down at my ring and I see this giant hunk of skin lodged between the J and the T. It was so big I actually had to pry it out of there! NASTY! (laughs)

I even told my mom that story, and a few others about nights that I used it. "You know Mom, this ring has really saved me a lot." (laughs)

Close Call at Questions

I've been blessed, man. I've had an angel looking over me because I've never once been stabbed, never got thrown in jail... although I did almost get shot once.

I was at a club called Questions, which was owned by one of my best friends. That night was actually an after party for one of my fights. I was never a bouncer there but I knew all the bouncers, so if things got bad, I would help out.

That night, this bouncer named James, a huge guy who had won the Mr. Florida contest, he has some dude in a headlock. Suddenly, he starts yelling to me, *"JERRY, GET HIM! HE'S GOT MY NUTS!"* So I start kicking the guy — *WHAM, WHAM* — and he eventually lets go and scurries away.

I follow the guy out into the parking lot, but then a car comes screeching up and the door pops open. I see a guy who must have been friends with the guy we kicked out, and he looks at me and says, "Fuck you, motherfucker!" and I see that he's got a gun!

There's people all around and he's got a girl [in the car], so I figure he's not gonna do anything — which is the STUPIDEST thing I could have thought. I actually said, "FUCK YOU. If you're gonna shoot me, shoot me! You ain't got the balls to shoot me!" He looks at me for a moment longer, then finally shuts the door and drives away.

A second later, I'm standing there and thinking, "Wow, that was DUMB. That wasn't smart at all!" (laughs)

🐦 *@JerryTrimble*

📷 *@jerry_trimble_*

🕸 *www.jerrytrimble.com*

Chapter Six

TY OLSSON

Photo courtesy Ty Olsson.

"I'm repeatedly smashing a guy's head into a soap dispenser while John and I argue over whether I'm justified for doing it."

A competitive martial artist, dancer, musician, and one of Canada's busiest actors, the multifaceted Ty Olsson has appeared in well over 150 film and television productions including *Battlestar Galactica* (as Capt. Aaron Kelly), *The 100* (as Grounder healer Nyko), and the smash-hit series *Supernatural* (as vampiric anti-hero Benny Lafitte).

Of particular note is Olsson's portrayal of retired MMA fighter Vic Carboneau in the sadly-mothballed series pilot *Borealis* (aka *Survival Code*), which was hailed by critics as one of the best pilots to come along in several years.

SHAMELESS MAULER SELF-PLUG: I coordinated and co-supervised the film's climactic fight scene between Olsson and fellow When We Were Bouncers alumnus Darren Shahlavi

But before he was an onscreen healer, soldier, vampire, or MMA champion, Olsson was just a strange-looking teenager working in one of Quebec's most outrageously violent party districts.

Thunderdome

During the early 90s I worked at a place called Thunderdome in Hull, Quebec, a short cab ride across the Ontario border from Ottawa.

The thing about Hull that made it unique was that it had a strip about a mile long with maybe twenty-five bars on it. It also had liquor licenses that allowed bars to stay open until 3 AM, and a drinking age of eighteen. Now, in Ontario, the legal age is nineteen and the bars close at one, so you'd have all these eighteen-year-olds from the colleges and universities in Ottawa heading over to Hull at the beginning of the night, followed later by people who'd do last call in Ottawa and then cross the border to drink for two more hours.

The strip became very notorious for its nightlife, and also for its fighting. People there were all young and stupid, so they'd drink their faces off and then come out into a big courtyard section of the strip and have gigantic fights. It would happen every weekend without fail, so much so that a lot of people who frequented the strip considered that a part of every night's entertainment. You'd drink yourself silly, go outside and grab yourself a shawarma or whatever, and watch the fights. Sometimes you could even watch two or three completely unrelated fights going on at once.

My bar, Thunderdome, was pretty much the only alternative [music] bar on the strip. They'd play stuff like Pearl Jam, Rage Against the Machine, and so forth, which very few clubs were playing at the time. Ironically, we also had the least trouble, because the freak crowd usually just wanted to party, not to fight. But every once in a while you'd get people who'd come in from one of the other bars, and sometimes they weren't a very good fit for Thunderdome. And then you'd have yourself a situation.

At this time I was around eighteen or nineteen, with a completely shaved head except for this kind of a braid hanging down the back. Before that, I used to have long hair, but one day I decided to shave the whole thing except for the braid, so I ended up looking like a fucked-up Hare Krishna. I was also playing city league football so I was training like a madman, full of testosterone. In a nutshell, I was a 205-pound nineteen-year-old with a funny haircut and a chip on his shoulder.

In addition to bouncing at night, I was spending my days working at a group home for troubled teens. Yeah, somehow I got the job at that age and with that haircut — don't ask me how because I still have no fucking idea. (laughs) So anyway, on one particular Canada Day [July 1st] I had to pull a long shift at the group home until ten at night. It was a drawn-out, pissy day with the kids being shitheads all day long, and to make things worse, I had to go straight from the home to start a shift at Thunderdome.

At around midnight, I was standing at my post and hating my life when I overheard this big guy giving one of the other bouncers a hard time. I picked up from the conversation that the bouncer had already bought the guy a beer as a way of trying to cool things off, but the guy was continuing to lip. Now, in spite of my appearance, I was actually known as a minimally-violent, "talk guys out of the bar" kind of bouncer. But with this dude acting like one of the kids I'd had to put up with for thirteen hours, it wasn't long before I'd had enough.

I walked over, grabbed the guy and said, "Just fuckin' relax! He bought you a beer, so grab a seat and chill the fuck out!" Of course that just made him start beakin' at me, "Blah, blah, blah, fuck you," and so forth. Well... that was the wrong day for him to do that. (laughs)

I finally looked at him and said, "You just won the jackpot," and then NAILED him with the best elbow strike I've ever thrown to this day. Even though he was four or five inches taller than me I actually knocked him up and onto the bar, and while he was sprawled over it, I drilled him one more time and then punted him in the face as he slid to the floor.

Like I said, I was known as one of the calmer guys on staff, so all the other bouncers couldn't believe the sight of "the calm guy" going apeshit and screaming at this dude's unconscious body! (laughs) When I finally calmed down, we dragged the guy into the alley out back and left him there, and when we came back in, I saw that he'd left a puddle of blood on the floor the size of a manhole cover! We all stood there looking at it for a second, waiting for somebody to volunteer to clean it up, until I finally just put a barstool over top of it and walked away.

Fuck it, cleanup ain't my job. I'm a bouncer.

Hare Krishna Superman

A few nights later I had a night off, and went out on the Ontario side with my brother Scott who's a total freaking madman. Seriously, that guy's got more violent stories than any five normal guys put together — so you can pretty much tell where this story's headed! (laughs)

Ottawa's a funny place. Because it's the center of government for Canada, everyone thinks of it as this pristine, pretty little city. But what people don't realize is that it's surrounded by all these butt-fuck redneck towns, so any time you go outside of the city, you meet all the craziest rednecks.

On this particular night, me, my brother and a few friends do some pre-drinking and then go to Kanata, a suburb-ey outskirt town outside of Ottawa. There was a hockey arena/fitness club there, and we had heard that someone got a special license to turn it into a booze garden for the night. So we walk in the door about an hour before the place is scheduled to close, and I'm wearing a plaid shirt with the sleeves cut off and my dumbass braid on the back of my head. While I'm not necessarily *looking* for trouble, by virtue of my appearance I'm pretty much a total aggro-magnet.

Now, Ottawa had a problem with steroids at the time, they were really, really rampant. I didn't take 'em, but almost everybody I knew did. Any club you went to, you could count on at least fifty percent of the guys there being on the juice. So we're walking past one such group when a really big, tall musclehead steps in front of my buddy Carl, who's a sweetheart of a guy and couldn't fight to save his life. Musclehead looks down at Carl and says, "Get out of my way!" as if Carl had somehow caused the guy to block his path. And with me already being drunk, it's an immediate pissing contest.

Ty (left) and me lookin' dead sexy on THE 100.

Being the hero that I think I am in my head (laughs), I shove Carl out of the way and begin lipping off to this big juice monkey. I even pull what was a regular move for me at the time and tell the guy my name. That was my thing, to announce who I was before a fight so that guys could warn their friends about me after I kicked their ass. I know, really smart, right? (laughs) But anyway, before things can kick off, Scott comes up behind me and whispers, "Ty — *no fighting!* I got us set up with free drinks after the bar closes!" As soon as I hear that, it's like a switch is flipped. Free drinks beat a fist fight any day, so I immediately shut up and walk away leaving a confused musclehead in my wake.

Ten minutes later I go to the bathroom and, seeing that all the urinals are in use, I go into a stall. I'm not in there very long before I hear the bathroom door open and the shuffling of multiple feet, and then a voice bellows out, *"WHICH ONE OF YOU IS TY OLSSON?!"*

Fuck. (laughs)

Now, a smart guy in these circumstances would stay hidden in the stall and hope for the best, right? But since I'm drunk and cocky and immortal, I shake my dick off, zip up, and come strutting out of the stall to face this big freaking mob of steroid guys that's filling up the room. Of course I don't care because I'm Drunken Hare Krishna Superman, so I start mouthing off again, yap, yap, yap.

I get about ten words out before this gigantic steroid monster, even bigger than the guy I had the original beef with, hauls off and hits me with the HARDEST punch that I've ever taken in my life! He just fuckin' SMOKES me, drives me five feet straight back into the stall! Thankfully for me, when you're nineteen and drunk you don't feel stuff like that until after, so I come storming right back out and wade into those guys.

Now I'm fucked. I'm dishing out licks to anyone I can reach, but I'm WAY outnumbered and it's not looking good at all. My only saving grace is that while all this is going on, someone is tipping my brother off about how The Steroid Patrol followed me into the bathroom. So of course he comes roaring down the hallway to help me out, but as he reaches the bathroom door, he finds a bouncer who's buddies with the Super Juice Friends blocking the doorway and saying, "You can't go in."

Right. One *WHAM* later, my brother's through the door.

As is the case with most mobs, if you have thirteen guys fighting, only maybe six are really into it, so as my brother gets stuck in and things get uglier, about half of the mob starts piling out. But it's still a savage mess, even after a bouncer friend of mine named John Stewart comes into the room to try to stop the insanity.

At that point I'm repeatedly smashing a guy's head into a soap dispenser, while John's trying to stop me and hold off the remaining juice monkeys at the same time. And the whole time that I'm slamming this guy's head, me and John are having a back-and-forth argument over whether I'm justified for doing it! (laughs)

Suddenly, one of the many hands grabbing me takes a hold of my stupid Hare Krishna ponytail and pulls my head down. Since I don't wanna be eating a bunch of knees and uppercuts, I reach up blindly and grab a handful of my attacker's hair, and then start giving solid licks in a full-blown hockey fight. Me and the other guy are just THROWING, each landing about five hard shots before I suddenly hear John yelling, *"TY! NO! IT'S YOUR BROTHER!"*

Um... what? (laughs)

I stop, look up, and sure enough I've been slugging it out with Scott! We both let this sink in for a moment, and then look around to see that the juice-heads have all taken off. Aside from me, Scott and John, the room is completely empty!

What a couple of morons! (laughs)

 @TyOlsson
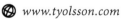 *www.tyolsson.com*

Chapter Seven

SCOTTY RIGGS

Photo courtesy Scotty Riggs

"No one wants to see a naked guy in the club,
but sometimes that bare ass has to be seen."

After breaking into the pro wrestling business in 1992, Scott Antol aka Scotty Riggs began his career in a number of southern-state independent organizations before signing with powerhouse World Championship Wrestling (WCW) in 1995.

In WCW, Riggs partnered with Marcus Alexander Bagwell to form the tag team of "The American Males," who feuded with world tag team champions Harlem Heat and briefly reigned as champions themselves. Riggs' eventual split with Bagwell was followed by a singles feud with former Extreme Championship Wrestling (ECW) superstar Raven.

After leaving WCW in 2000, Riggs worked in ECW as Scotty Anton, then plied his trade in AWA and several independent groups before retiring in 2009.

Tangling with a Scorpion

When I was still in high school, in the summer of 1984 or '85, I got a job working at a series of rock concerts. It was really cool, I got to work at [shows featuring] a bunch of great rock bands and some cool country acts. One night I was working a show that had Krokus, Bon Jovi and Def Leppard. At the beginning of the night we were standing backstage sorting out where we needed to be and stuff. I looked at this guy standing next to me and saw that he had this big, crazy hairdo and eye makeup on. When he finally walked away, I turned to the nearest [bouncer] and said, "Who's that fag that was standing next to me?" He said, "Dude, that was Jon Bon Jovi!" (laughs) I look back now and shake my head — here's this teenaged kid, this clueless moron calling Jon Bon Jovi a fag!

One night at a Scorpions concert, I was facing the crowd with my back against the stage. At one point a microphone cable came flying over the edge of the stage and kind of got hooked on me, and then somebody started pulling on it. So I started pulling back, trying to get loose. I finally got it off me and let it go, just as the other person yanked on it HARD. That other person ended up being Klaus Meine, lead singer of the Scorpions, and the cable we were both pulling on flew up and hit him right in the face! (laughs)

Sending a Message

Later on I started bouncing at this strip club, a little place in Atlanta. I had just started wrestling, and [WCW/WWE wrestler] Steve Regal — they call him William Regal, now — was teaching me. I ended up using a lot of the ideas he told me about wrestling to deal with John Q. Public as well. The number one thing that stuck in my head was, "If anybody starts getting rough with you, if somebody ever pisses you off, don't hit 'em or fight 'em. Just take your thumb and stick it in their eye." While I didn't try to blind every guy I had a problem with at the bar, I did use that mentality of beating my opponents to the punch by going after them ten times harder than they came after me.

One night I heard something going on in one of the back rooms, and I looked in to see that this Mexican dude was screwing a dancer, who of course was getting extra money to do it. I went over and hammer-locked the guy, pinned his hand up behind his back with his thumb almost touching his ear, and then got a handful of hair with my other hand. He didn't have a whole lot of fight in him — his pants were down around his ankles so he had no legs — and I dragged him all the way through the club with his business flopping around for everyone to see. Nobody wants to see a naked guy in the club, but sometimes that bare ass has to be seen, just to send a message! (laughs)

Battling Belligerent Brits

I moved on to work at a piano bar in Hilton Head, South Carolina. The bartender had been serving Jagermeister to these English guys, and they were HAMMERED. Now, I don't know if you know this, but when English people get hammered, they get belligerent. They drink and they want to fight, it's just their persuasion.

The bartender cut 'em off, and after they started raising a ruckus, he somehow managed to get one of 'em outside on his own. I happened to be standing out front, just off to the side of the door, and I saw the bartender and the one guy come out [but didn't know] that there was another guy coming too.

The first English dude spit on the bartender and then ran like hell, leaving us both giggling over what a tough guy he was to spit-and-run like that. But then the other guy came out and coldcocked the bartender from behind, just cheap-shotted 'im. I guess he was thinking he was gonna do a hit-and-run of his own, but he didn't know that I was standing right there.

This was before UFC got real big, and nobody believed that the pro wrestling sleeper hold was real. Of course, now that everybody's seen it used in real fights as the rear-naked choke, they know it really works. I put it on the English guy and squeezed until his face turned purple. Then he started snoring and his eyes rolled up in his head, so that's when I knew that it was time to let go. (laughs) I let him down to the ground, and when he started waking up and moving, I locked his arms up in a catch wrestling hook called a sugar hold. He eventually woke up all the way and started screaming, "You're breaking my arm! You're breaking my arm!" So I told him, "If you move, I WILL break your arm." With what I'd learned from Regal I could've broken both of 'em actually, and without even breaking a sweat.

There was probably about seventy-five people watching this, and I was glad for that because the spitter had gone and got the cops. But when they got there, the crowd all backed my version of the story and it was the English guys who ended up getting arrested! (laughs) We had to go to court shortly after, and my bartender still had a black eye while the English dudes didn't have a mark on 'em, so after hearing the whole story, the judge actually applauded me for not seriously injuring that English guy. I couldn't have written a better script for how it played out.

I ended up getting a huge reputation off that incident, and that caused people to not want to cause trouble at my bar. From then on, my job was easy because the word had went out, "Don't mess with this guy. He *knows* shit." All I had to do was lay a hand on somebody's shoulder to get 'em to settle right down, and that bar became the most peaceful place. Girls felt safe coming there, so I met a lot more chicks after that, too. It worked out well that way. (laughs)

That's why all bouncers should know some basic grappling moves. It's amazing what kind of a message you can send if you can control your emotions and have a little bit of training. You can get the job done without having to do any real damage.

🐦 *@realscottyriggs*

Chapter Eight

JAMES "THE SLEDGEHAMMER" McSWEENEY

All photos courtesy James McSweeney.

"He turns and I just head-kick him, take his head pretty much completely off."

One of the baddest mamma-jammas ever to come out of the UK, James "The Sledgehammer" McSweeney has a ridiculous amount of combat credentials under his belt.

A six-time world Muay Thai champion and three-time world heavyweight MMA champ, McSweeney gained widespread notoriety with his appearance on The Ultimate Fighter reality show, where he justified being first overall pick during team selections with victories over gargantuan NFL veterans Wes Shivers and Matt "Meathead" Mitrione.

Outside of the UFC, The Sledgehammer has competed in a number of elite fighting groups including Singapore's ONE FC, Poland's KSW, and Japan's legendary K-1 kickboxing organization. Recently retired from competition, he now operates his McSweeney Fight Factory school on Australia's Gold Coast, and promotes combat sport events under the LEGEND MMA banner.

Bloody Business at Bagley's

I worked at some pretty bad places in London. People trying to stab us, shoot at us, trying to run me over and such. One of the toughest places I ever worked was called Bagley's, in King's Cross in the West End of London. It used to be an old film studio, but it got bought out by a crime family who re-opened it as a nightclub. This was in the early 2000s, which was a rough time in London with all kinds of things going on. People getting attacked, drugged, date-raped and so on.

Bagley's had three sound stages that were turned into rooms that played different types of music. There was first a hard house room, then an R&B room in the middle, and then the far one was a techno room. So you'd get very different kinds of crowds in the place at the same time — there'd be a drug crowd in the hard house room, in the R&B room would be darker crowd with more black guys, and then in the techno room a lot of metal guys who wore black, gothic-style [clothes]. Three different crowds that didn't mix very well at all — in fact they pretty much seemed to hate each other! They all had separate bathrooms, but they had to walk through each other's rooms to get to their bathrooms so there was always trouble.

We used to run an undercover drug squad in each room, who'd stand up above the lights on wooden-floored scaffolding that couldn't be seen from the dance floor. They'd carry these little red laser pointers that fire for miles, like you'd see on the top of a gun, and any time they spotted trouble or a drug deal going down or something, they'd just hit [the people involved] with that little red laser, and the team on the ground would see it and come and get you.

On one occasion I was outside the front doors taking a break, and there was a guy out there who I'd sent away earlier. He kept coming back, being a real nuisance. [From the start] his attitude had been very aggressive. At first, my guys were thinking maybe they were gonna let him in anyway, but I said, "No, I'm not having it." One guy on his own, coming to a pub like this, it was very strange anyway. And then when he started being so aggressive to a whole team of big guys at a problem club... I mean, our security team had a reputation. Not of being heavy-handed, but just for not being a team that you'd mess with. You wouldn't talk to these [doormen] so aggressive for no reason, especially when they were genuinely trying to ask you a question, so for this guy to get aggressive so quick, it just didn't make sense. Either he was on something or he had a problem, and either way I didn't want him coming in.

Now it was his fourth time coming back, and he kept yelling more and more threats. I decided that enough was enough, and me and a couple of my guys went to escort him off [the premises]. This club had a long, long runway going from the front door to the main street that was very badly lit. There was no cameras out there either, so it was a real hotspot for a lot of problems — like the one we were about to have.

I went to grab the guy, but he turned to me and pulled something out of his jacket. My instant, normal reaction was that it was a knife, because stabbings were very common in that area. But instead, I saw a big 5 ml [syringe] full of red! This guy's screaming his head off that he's going to kill me while he's trying to poke me with the needle, *"I'll fucking inject you with HIV, you piece of shit! You're gonna get AIDS!"*

My guys were always pretty switched-on — this was a pretty bad area and they expected things like this to happen — so they immediately started to circle around and get to his back so they could grab him or hit him or do something else to stop the situation. Meanwhile, I looked at the guy and said, "Okay, if you're going to do it, then do it! Don't keep talking, stab me with it!" Of course I really didn't think he had it in him to do it. You don't wave a [syringe] around, you just stab someone with it if you're going to stab them. You don't try to show everybody, or shout off that you've got something if you're really going to do it. So I kind of didn't believe he was serious, or that [the liquid in the syringe] was really what he said it was.

Now he's getting more erratic and more crazy, and I'm backing away while he comes forward, still swinging this big pump around. Then he starts getting the gist that people are getting behind him, so he's turning around fast and he's threatening everybody. At that point he's got three or four guys around him, so whichever way he turns, he's got his back to at least one of us.

As he turns and turns, I think, "Next time he turns his back to me, I'm gonna get him." Then he turns his head to the left and I know that I'm out of his vision, so I just head-kick him, take his head pretty much completely off. I really step into it, give it everything I have, shin-kicking him right across the top of the head. And it knocks him clean unconscious — he went out BAD. I jumped straight on him to hit him again because I wasn't going to take the chance [of him still being awake], but then I saw for certain that he was unconscious. So

I grabbed the needle, wrapped it in tissue, and kept it to one side for [evidence].

When the police came, they were very unhappy because he was marked up from where I'd kicked him and from when he landed pretty heavy on his head. But once I explained the situation they calmed down a little bit, and after they took the evidence and our statements, they got the guy and left.

The following week, the officers came back for follow-up questioning. By that time they had the blood [test] results back — the blood in the syringe had tested positive for HIV, and the guy who was swinging it around had it in his bloodstream as well! It was so lucky that I smelled a rat from the beginning, and we didn't let the guy in the club. Who knows how many people in there could have got injected with HIV?

Pissed-Off Gypsy

About a year before that, when I was nineteen or twenty, I was running a club in Wickham, back in Barkshire. We had a thing called Pubwatch, where if you were barred from one pub, you were barred from them all. All the doormen in town would have these radios and if someone got thrown out, everybody else would get the message to not let that person in on that particular evening.

One night, we were pre-warned that this guy had been a nuisance throughout that whole night through many different bars. I think his name was Carl something. His family were a traveler family, which means that they were gypsies. When the travelers are in town, there's always a problem — they always get drunk, they always start fights, they always want to prove themselves. Every one thinks they're a boxer, and this particular guy was thought to be one of the better ones, the top dog in his family. So everywhere he went, there was a fucking problem. We knew the guy, and thought, "He's not even going to try coming to ours, he's going to go home." But a while later, here he comes down the street.

As he approaches, I walk out to him and tell him, "Listen, don't even come onto the premises. You know you're barred, you're on Pubwatch. Just go home. Wherever you go, nobody's going to let you in. You're already on the canvas." Of course he starts effin' and blindin', making threats like he's gonna come back and all the rest of it. I just said, "Don't come back and do it, just do it now! You threaten me you're gonna come back in an hour and beat me up? Just do it now!" But he keeps on about how he's gonna do this, and he's gonna do that, until eventually off he goes.

Bloodied but unbowed, McSweeney kicks Roger Gracie right inna face at a ONE FC event in Manila, Philippines.

Later on at about twelve-thirty, we're starting to close down the bar one area at a time, moving people into the main-area dance floor. Suddenly I get a call [on my radio]: *"CODE RED, CODE RED, FRONT DOOR!"* Code Red is [the signal for] the biggest problem you could have, so I run through the club to the front. And when I get there, all I can see is this big, fuck-off JCB [backhoe] belting toward the front doors! (laughs) All these wooden chairs and tables [on the patio] are being rolled over and crushed, like those big four-wheeler [monster trucks] in America that crush all the cars, you know?

He's belting toward the front door and I'm thinking, "He's gonna stop. He's just trying to scare everyone, he's gonna stop." But then I see that he's so close, and going so fast... he ain't gonna fucking stop. (laughs) Everyone just runs for cover, and he comes blasting right through the front door.

The way the club was set up, part of it was a building that was over a hundred years old, and then it had an extension built onto it that held the dance floor of the club. Well, this guy smashed right through the old part of the club, kept going all the way to the middle of the dance floor before he finally took his foot off the gas!

By sheer luck he actually didn't hit nobody, but half the place was now falling down and landing all around him. Quite a few people got injured from the falling debris of the building. There were people with cut heads from the ceiling falling on them, people who'd fallen down, people who'd been trampled or landed on broken glass... I think there was close to thirty or forty people who got injured out of four or five hundred in the club.

Then he run out of there through the back of the building, took off through the grass. Me and three of the other doormen chased after him and caught him down by the garden, and we pretty much kicked the shit out of him before dragging him back. I ended up putting his arm all the way up his back while holding him in a rear-naked choke with the arm trapped, made him pass out while we all carried him. We really had no choice because he tried to fight us all the way, he wouldn't come back without a fight. We had to give him a bit of a beating and restrain him, drag him all the way back and wait for the police to come and pick him up.

Garbage Day

In later years I worked at a club called The Stork Rooms in the West End, right by Piccadilly Circus. A guy named Piers Adam had paired up with Marco Pierre White, the guy who taught Gordon Ramsay how to cook, to open this place. A friend of mine got the contract for it and I was made head of security, but I was only going to do it for a short time until my friend could find someone more suitable for the job. I really didn't need to do that [job], I was just helping him out.

It was pretty much an easy place because it was invitation-only and everyone had to be on the guest list. Very low-key, the entrance was out of the way and it wasn't well-advertised. Paparazzi weren't allowed, very minimal security inside — a place where people can go and just do what they want. [The people who went there] weren't real celebrities, they weren't like Robert De Niro or anything. More like the Paris Hilton-kind of celebrities of England. Kind of socialites who think they're celebrities, but they're not really. Famous in the [nightclub] scene maybe, but not outside of it.

[The job] wasn't really a problem, but you had to have patience. Everyone thinks they're famous, everyone thinks they're on the list. One night this guy shows up, and I recognize him straight away from a movie that was very big at the time. He's about four hundred pounds, a big, fat black guy. He turns up, gets out of his car, then undoes the red rope out front and just walks in!

I'm talking to someone else when I notice this guy go barging past, so I grab his coat and he instantly spins around. *"Don't touch me! Don't put your fucking hands on me, don't you know who the fuck I am?"* and all this. I said to him, "I don't give a fuck who you are, you don't walk through my ropes. Now get the fuck back." I push him back, put him behind the ropes and say, "Alright, let's have some manners. What's your name?"

But instead, he proceeds to tell me that he's mad as fuck, and that he knows Piers Adam and he's gonna get me fired and all this shit. I say, "Just let me know your name. I'll get the girl here to look on the list, and if you're name's on it, I'm gonna let you in." Because even when you've already been an asshole, when you've already been rude and sworn at me and I don't wanna let you in, if you're on the list then I have to. I have to swallow my pride.

A guy who's with him says, "He's an actor," and I say, "Mate, I know who he is. I recognize him. But I don't know his name, tell me his name." And he finally tells me. So I check with the girl, and the name's not on the list. To be honest, I'm kind of happy about that. (laughs) So I say, "Listen, you're not on the list, so that's it. You're not gonna come in. Even if you did know the owners of this club, I don't think they'd let you treat their club or their staff this way. So that's it."

Straight away, he gets on the phone and starts swearing to someone on the [other end], telling them that they better come down there and take care of me, telling me that I'm not gonna make it home safe tonight. He's saying that he may be an actor but he's also a gangster, and he's gonna do all these nasty things to me. Finally, he shuts the phone off and tells me to stay there and wait 'cause there's people coming for me. So I tell him, "Okay, I'm here all night. I'm here till three in the morning. Let's just wait."

Fifteen, twenty minutes go by, and he's still standing there waiting while his mate's trying to get him to leave. "Come on, fuck this guy. Let's go and have a good night somewhere else. You earn more in an hour than he does in a month. Come on, let's walk away." And eventually the guy does, he starts to walk away — but as he walks past me, he turns and spits straight in my face! I should have seen it coming, but I thought he was just going to say something stupid.

The Sledgehammer rockin' his FFF world mixed martial arts title.

And now he's standing there with his face about a foot away from mine, and I can feel this phlegm on my cheek.

Well, I just lost my temper and flew at him. Ended up hittin' him — I think I head-butted him and hit him with a couple of punches, and he went down. I went a little bit overboard, to be honest. Beat him up maybe a little bit more than I should've done. His friend ran off and left him, and he ended up lying unconscious in the street.

It's a one-way road in front of that club, just a single, narrow street, and now there's all this traffic and no one can get through because of the big, four-hundred-pound black guy laying in the middle of the road! (laughs) And no one's helping me [to move him]! I've only got the little girl working the front counter inside, and I can't lift this fucking guy!

At this point I'm kind of laughing to myself, because in the movie that this guy was in, his character was in the same situation and someone said, "Just leave that guy there, you won't be able to lift him." And now I'm in the same role as the guys in the movie! (laughs) Fuck's sake. I'm trying to get him to wake up but he won't wake up, so I roll him all the way across to the other side of the road. Took me almost five minutes, and I was well out of breath by the time I finished.

Now, in London, at nighttime everyone puts their black [garbage] bins out from the bars and the restaurants, and then the dustbin drivers come along and pick 'em up with their truck. So there's like, thirty black bin liners [garbage bags] filled with rubbish and crap piled up across from the club. Since I don't want to get in trouble and have the police come, I start putting the bin liners all on top of the guy to cover him up! (laughs) He's still not waking up, but I check and I can tell he's still breathing.

About fifteen minutes later, I'm back on the door and he still hasn't moved. We're about twenty minutes from closing and I just want to get out of there. But then Piers Adam turns up with his security and his driver and his little entourage. He asks me how the night went, and I tell him there's been no real issues. Then he says, "Oh by the way, I forgot to put him on the list, but [the big guy's name] will be coming down. He's a friend of mine, so make sure you let him in, won't you?"

Shit! (laughs)

I say, "Uh... yeah, no problem. If he turns up I'll send him right through," and Piers goes inside just as I start to hear moaning coming up from the pile of rubbish across the street! (laughs)

Then the guy's friends come back and it's kicking off, they're yelling, "Where's our boy?" and that. So I tell them, "He's over there, he's under those bin liners. You'd better go and pick him up." They wake him up but he doesn't know where he is, he's not with it, and at that point I go inside because it's finally time to close up.

I know it's only a matter of time before the big boy remembers what happened, so I walk straight over to Piers and say, "Piers, I have to go. I've got to be up early in the morning to train. Are your people okay to close up?" He tells me sure, just lock up on my way out, and straight away I'm out the door and driving off.

So, yeah... they fired me. (laughs)

Putting It Behind Me

While I was back in England for my UFC 120 fight, my wife threw me a surprise birthday party. All my old security friends turned up, and as all the old stories came out, I realized that while some of them seem really funny now, at the time they were very serious.

To be honest, it's not funny that I bashed a guy because he spat in my face. I'm not proud that I beat that guy up and put him in the bins, but at the time, that's the way I dealt with things. Back in those days, I was a lot younger, wilder, I had a lot more faster temper. When you work security every day and every night, your tolerance level starts to get thinner and thinner and thinner because you put up with one arsehole after another, every single night. Whereas now, I can't remember the last time I had a street fight.

You become so much more mellow [with time]. I've become a family man now, I've got a wife and a baby. Things have changed, and I really try to put that side of my life far behind me. I'm not the same person I used to be. We all mature, and our circumstances become different.

One of the big reasons that I decided to leave England was because I was caught up in that nightlife and that security scene. I was a professional fighter and I ran a big security firm of close to 150 guys across London every night. With that comes a lot of different opportunities [to get into] a lot of different things on that side of life, and it's good to leave all that kind of things behind. Now I live a clean, honest life. A family life. I'm a sportsman and an athlete and I'm doing a job that is my dream, as opposed to a job that I had to do to get to my dream.

When you do tell a story about those days, people always see the end result, like, "You hurt the guy, that's a terrible thing." And of course it is a terrible thing, but you know what? If you didn't hurt him, then he would have hurt you first. You wasn't the person to throw the first punch, or the first one to use an implement. If you show any weakness out there, they'll be all over you like a pack of lions.

It was a different life back then. A different mindset, a different age and stage when you do those kinds of things. I met some amazing friends, and I went through some great highs and some great lows. I look back and see so many close calls, and only through skill, and luck, and God — all of the above — did I get through it in one piece.

I can laugh now because that's a way of dealing with it, a way that helps me to sleep better at night. But really, I feel like I'm very blessed to get through that stage of my life, and I'd hate to look back now and try to glorify it.

@mcsweeneymma

66

Chapter Nine

NOAH DALTON DANBY

Photo courtesy DavidLeyes.com

"The doors were bending and bowing from people wanting to come in and kill us!"

Many actors can only play at being badasses, but Noah Dalton Danby backs it up with real-life experience.

A high-level practitioner of the violent art of hapkido, Danby is also trained in Greco-Roman wrestling and has well over a decade of experience bouncing in his dual home bases of Toronto and Vancouver.

Despite boasting an ever-expanding resume that includes *Orphan Black, Stargate SG-1, The 100, Bitten,* and the Vin Diesel sci-fi actioner *Riddick*, Danby continues to work as a bouncer at various high-end Toronto nightclubs — presumably because he's one of those action-junkie maniacs who get bored if they go too long without rolling the dice with their well-being.

An Ultra-Violent Start

When I first moved to Toronto to go to Ryerson Theater school, I needed a job to support me so I started working the door. I started at Vinnie's Pub, in downtown Toronto at Duncan and Adelaide. They had $2.50 highballs, so it got a little crazy. One night I saw a bouncer throw a guy onto a pool table, then pick up a billiard ball and start hitting him in the face with it. It was a little insane.

There was a bar across the street called The Limelight. Big nightclub in Toronto, had a lot of years under it. We were working one Sunday and [The Limelight was] just opening up. I guess they had crossed some gangsters of some sort, because just after they'd opened the doors, all these guys drove up in their cars, got out with pipes, and laid the beats to one of the doormen! The other guys got inside, but [the guy who was beaten] ended up in a coma for over three months. He was never the same again. That was one of the most violent things that I saw at the beginning of my bouncing career.

I learned a lot from a guy named Jason Taylor, he's still one of my best friends now. Jason came to work at Vinnie's within a week of my starting. He had done a lot of bouncing, and he started running the door while I was the young buck working inside. I learned a lot there, what to do and what not to do.

One night, one of our bouncers — a giant of a guy, like, six-six — picked up this little guy who was mouthin' off to him and dragged him out into the alley. The big guy didn't have to do anything else, but he took out his pepper spray anyway and sprayed the little guy in the face! Just buried that spray right in his face and threw him down. The little guy was crying, choking, and when it was finally all over, Jason looked at me and said, "Now, THAT'S excessive." (laughs)

This was around 1995, during the last few years when the police were really on our side. They'd squash instances like that one, you know, nobody was getting charged. They'd take [an angry customer] aside and say, "Listen, buddy, here's the deal. This is what's gonna happen — you're gonna charge [the bouncer], it's gonna go to court, you won't win because they'll prove you were intoxicated, and it's gonna be a big waste of everybody's time." So most of the time, the police would squash things no matter how bad they were.

Mea Maxima Culpa

I moved on to a couple of other places before I eventually made the jump to a big super-club called Whiskey Saigon, just up the street from Vinnie's. It was this bizarre place with three levels.

The first level was a loungey-type area where they played kind of a house mix. I remember [sportscaster] Ron Maclean coming in there, all the stars would come in and hang out on that level. The second level was like the alternative, where everybody would smoke pot and listen to thrasher music. And the third level was this insane sort of techno level. They'd play stuff like "Rhythm is a Dancer" or "I'm a Barbie Girl", it was in that era.

What made this probably the craziest club I ever worked at was that at two o'clock, they'd shut down the alternative floor and every-body would move up [to the third level]. You'd get this real clash of personalities happening — skater punks trying to mix with house guys. It just wouldn't mesh, and we had some major brawls happen there, just huge. But the biggest one by far was one that I started. (laughs)

We used to have these trannies come in, there were three of them, and you couldn't tell [that they were men]. They were beautiful... guys. (laughs) They'd wear collars to cover their Adam's apples, and their hands were pretty decent, looked like fairly feminine hands. If you didn't know in advance what they were, I could see how you might not figure it out. And their thing was to take a guy and blow him in the girls' washroom. Sometimes we'd stop them... and sometimes we wouldn't. (laughs)

So this busload of people comes in from Barrie [Ontario], and that's already a recipe for disaster, right? One of the trannies takes one of the [Barrie] guys into the washroom, and I nudge my buddy Peter and say, "Hey Peter, watch this." Then I go over to this band of Barrie guys who think their boy's gone in to get a blowjob from a hot Asian chick, and I go, "Hey — that's a GUY."

Now the whole group is going, "Oh my God, what do we do?" and one of the guys gets up to go stop 'em. But right away, another guy grabs him and says, "No! No! You can't stop it!" (laughs) Eventually, their friend comes out with a big, smug smile on his face. Then the Asian trannie comes out wiping his lips off, grabs his two girls — or guys, or whatever — and they get out of there. Everybody's laughing at the guy [who got blown] and he can't understand why — until they tell him. He's like, "No! No!" but they all point at me, and I'm nodding my head up and down like, "Yes! Yes!" (laughs)

Then he starts to FLIP OUT. His friends are trying to calm him down but he's out of control. Finally, somebody bumps into him and he just hauls off and punches the guy! So now the friends of the guy who got punched are pushing and shoving with the busload from Barrie, and they all just empty into the street. The guy who got blown is so mad that there's tears coming out of his eyes, he just wants to hit things. So he runs over to a hot dog cart and smashes the hot dog guy in the face!

Now, that was a BIG mistake, because those hot dog guys are probably the most lethal guys. Sure enough, when the cart got tipped over, a gun fell out onto the street! Our manager Rob quickly picked up the gun, gave it to the hot dog guy and said, "You've gotta get out of here because this is gonna get ugly." Then Rob turns around and smacks the blowjob guy, and since Rob was our captain, that meant it was ON.

[Our crew] went two-by-two into the street, just as other bars across from us like Fluid and The Big Easy were emptying out. The street became a literal flood of people hitting each other, and I paired up with a bouncer named Jay Lagarde, a scrappy little Asian dude.

Danby and the Maxim girls. Bouncing doesn't always suck.
(Photo courtesy Noah Dalton Danby)

He would hit a guy, then bolt to the right, and as the guy looked over at Jay to hit him back, I'd nail the dude and finish him off. We just worked our way through the crowd like that, knocking guys out left, right and center. But then we got swarmed and pushed back through the doors [of our club]. After the last of our guys was inside, we closed the doors, locked 'em, and held 'em shut. The doors were bending and bowing from people wanting to come in and kill us!

Eventually, we saw cherries [police lights], heard sirens and cops on a megaphone, and it finally dissipated.

Man, that was absolute chaos... AND I STARTED IT! (laughs)

Playing the Fame Card

One night, a singer named Alannah Myles came to the door. She was really popular at the time, had a top-ten song called "Love Is" and a few others. I remember that broad coming up to the door and pulling the old, "Don't you know who I am?" routine. I HATE that shit. My ex-wife pulled that once in LA and I just put my head down in shame, like, "FUCK." Later, I went back to the guy [at the door] and apologized. I told him, "I'm so sorry. I know your job is tough and you don't deserve that." And he's like, "Thanks, man... your wife's a bitch." (laughs)

You Lookin' at My Girl?

I eventually got fired from Whiskey Saigon. In fact, the whole security team got gutted. They said we were taxing people too much [at the door], so when the bar started tanking, they thought it was us. And it's true, it might have been us. (laughs) So they brought in a private security team, and we all had to go elsewhere.

I ended up as the only white guy at an all-black club. One night I was in the VIP room, and this beautiful girl walked by. I kind of followed her with my eyes and looked at her bum, and when I turned back around, there's a dude standing there who pulls out a gun and jams it in my stomach!

He goes, "You like what you see?! That's my girl!" and I say, "No!" So he goes, "What, you *DON'T* like her?!" (laughs) I said, "No, she's very beautiful, but I wasn't trying to be disrespectful at all." A moment goes by, and then he puts his gun away, smiles, and says, "Aw, I was just fuckin' with you."

I go straight over to the owner, this guy named Moses, and tell him what happened. But he just laughs and goes, "Oh, that's just so-and-so" as if it's nothing!

Needless to say, I quit on the spot. (laughs)

Madonna and Fassbender

I remember doing security for the Toronto Film Festival, and they put me on Michael Fassbender's security team. This was just after he did [the feature film] *300,* but he hadn't become as big as he is now. I told him, "I can appreciate what you do, you're great," and he replied, "Cool — hey, let's go smoke a joint!" (laughs) I didn't hit it much, though — wouldn't have been able to do my job if I did.

Madonna was there as well. She got a bad rap because she didn't want anybody on the [security] staff looking at her. People hear that and they assume it's an ego thing, but it wasn't an ego thing. It was because there were so many people who came to see her... I mean, I've never seen such fame. It was like Jackie Chan, or Wayne Gretzky in Canada, just droves of people showing up to see her.

They didn't want anybody who was [on the security] staff looking at her because her private security, and our staff as well, had to be able to tell people apart in this sea of humanity. If you were looking at her for more than a moment, that's the first way to tell that you're not working for her. And if you really are working for her [and you're looking at her], you're not doing a good job of security because you need to be looking other places.

So yeah, don't look at Madonna — look at the crowd, look at the other people. I always thought she got a bad rap when I'd hear some of the security guys criticizing her over the radio.

The Lindros Brothers

One time I caught [NHL players] Eric and Brett Lindros doing drugs in a club bathroom. They'll deny it to this day. I know people who've brought it up to them and they say, "We weren't! We weren't!" But they were.

Actually, Eric wasn't. Eric was standing back while his friends and Brett were standing at a counter, and when I broke the washroom door open, one of them brushed a bunch of white powder onto the floor. So I said, "Okay, you guys are out," and Eric was the first to hold his hands up and say, "Okay, I'm out." But Brett made a big stink, because I don't think he wanted the heat going onto his brother. One of their friends was like a pitbull, he came at us swinging, so we put his head over a railing and dummied him a few times.

We got them all outside, and the pitbull guy was still freaking out. Then the cops came and they're like, "Hey, Brett!" So we thought, "Oh, we're fucked" because we hit [Brett's] friend. Then a cop goes over to the pitbull guy and says, "Hey man, take it easy," and puts a

When he was asked about this black eye, Danby's answer was concise: "Six of us, fourteen of them." (Photo courtesy Noah Dalton Danby)

hand on his shoulder. But the guy turns around and says, "Get your fuckin' hands off me, *PIG!*" and shoves the cop! Every single bouncer was like, *"YES!!!"* (laughs)

So we never caught any heat, and the cops took the guy away in a paddy wagon after they pepper sprayed the shit out of him! (laughs)

Adding Insult to Injury

One night, I was standing at the door when a black guy walked up to me, made a gun with his fingers and thumb and put [his hand] up to my head. Dug his fingers right into the side of my forehead and shoved my head sideways, letting me know — or wanting me to think, at least — that he was gonna shoot me.

You can't take stuff like that lightly, so I spun around and dropped him with my left hand. But when I hit him a second time while he was falling, my wrist was cocked at an awkward angle and I

76

sprained it. So now I'm fucking furious, but I can't hit the guy again because he's already unconscious.

But I was SO ANGRY, I needed to do something else to this guy. So as one of the other bouncers started dragging him away, I ran over and pulled his pants down to his knees. Underwear, too — left him lying there with his ass and dick hanging out! (laughs)

Well, the guy's girlfriend LOSES IT, and she runs up to me like she's gonna hit me. I get my hands up to block her punch, but she doesn't even get one off before this giant Serbian bouncer I work with steps in and — *BOOM!* — punches her right in the face!

She's out cold instantly, and I'm looking at the guy like, "What the fuck?" But he's not even looking at me, he's just screaming, *"IN MY COUNTRY, WOMAN DOES NOT DO THIS!!! IN MY COUNTRY, WOMAN KNOWS BETTER!!!"*

Jesus Christ! (laughs)

Checking out the 604

Moving to Vancouver for a while was fun. I bounced at The Roxy and it was a shit show, just a shit show. I'd get onstage and sing with the band and stuff like that. I wasn't getting any grease [bribes] from the door, so I was like, "Fuck it — if something happens, I'm there, but I'm also gonna have some fun." And the bar was totally okay with me having fun. I did my share of man-whoring, too — which was a pretty easy thing to do at The Roxy! (laughs)

I remember a guy causing trouble one night. He was a [good fighter] for sure because he went toe-to-toe with one of our bouncers and smoked him. So I shot in, grabbed his leg, worked my way up to his head, and head-and-arm [threw] him. But this guy knew what he was doing, and as we were falling, his hand went straight to my nuts. After we landed, he grabbed one of my nuts and just SQUEEZED.

Right away, I put two of my fingers deep in the guy's eye socket, hooked them in behind [the eyeball] and said, "I'm gonna pop this fucker out if you don't let go!" So of course he let go. I was about to let him go too, because I respected this guy for doing that, but then the bouncer that he had smoked — who was about six-foot-six — jumped as high as he could and stomped both feet down onto the guy's chest! I heard *POP-POP*, and knew immediately that he must have broken a couple of ribs.

So I jumped up, held the other bouncer off and said, "Dude, he's done! Don't worry about it!" Then I realized that here I was defending this guy, when just a few seconds earlier he was squeezing my balls while I was about to pop his eye out! (laughs)

Celebs at Global

Later on, I worked at a club called Global in Yaletown [an upscale district of downtown Vancouver]. One night an actor from *Six Feet Under*, Matthew St. Patrick, came in while I was at the door. It wasn't too busy and I was standing outside, learning lines for an audition. When he saw the lines in my hand, he said, "Hey, you want some help with your audition?" Of course I said, "Yeah, sure. Please." and he helped me with my lines and then gave me some things to do the next morning to prep. The next day I did exactly what he said, and I got the part! It was a big role, too — they flew me down to San Fran. Man, what a cool guy!

I had a moment like that with Gerard Butler, right after he did *300*. The movie hadn't come out yet, so this was before everybody knew who he was. He was really talkative, smoking like a chimney and talking about the film, even saying he was going to get me the graphic novel [that the movie was based on].

Years later I ended up doing security for him, but of course I didn't go up and say, "Hey man, remember me?" because I didn't expect him to. It was a red carpet event, and the crowd was so big and thick that I had to jump in and cut a person off who was trying to reach out and grab [Gerard]. But when I cut that person off, I also bumped Gerard, and he looked at me and said, "Maybe YOU'D like to walk the fuckin' red carpet!" I was like, "Wow, really?" (laughs) I mean, everyone has a bad day, but I was just trying to do a job, and I was doing it for him. And he was so nice to me before! I guess you never know.

Talking Over Fighting

It's getting a little hectic in Toronto lately. One buddy of mine named Andrew who I trained hapkido with was working at an after-hours club where he disallowed drugs in the bar. One night he kicked some guys out for it, and they went away, came back, put a gun up to the back of his head while he was talking to a girl, and blew his head off. It would be a tragedy anyway, but it's even more so because this guy was such an elite martial artist, so good with his hands. Such talent, just wasted.

That's why I've always been a bit of a talker. I can talk myself out of situations, talk people down. I find that people, when they get drunk, I can talk to them like they're kids. I'll rub their back a little bit and say, "Hey man, it's okay. It's okay." Sometimes part of me even wants them to react negatively to that, but most of the time, they don't. They actually like the feeling of having somebody comforting them.

Sticking Your Neck Out

One night at the club I work at now, three guys went outside and down the street a little bit, and they held another guy down and curb-stomped him. As soon as I see this, I run into the fray. There's a big group of people standing there and they all could have taken me down, but when I get there they just scatter. I start hitting and I drop one guy, and then I turn to the guy who jumped on the dude's head. He puts his hands up and goes, *"No, no, no, no!"* but I hit him anyway and he starts to fall. As he's falling, I bring my leg up and catch him right in the head with my shin. *BOOM!*

He goes down like he's been shot — like Randy Couture when he fought Lyoto Machida — and the guy's girlfriend is crying and screaming, *"WHAT DID YOU DO?!! WHAT DID YOU DO?!!"* Inside of me I'm thinking, "Yeah, what DID I do? Holy shit, holy shit!" but I stay calm for her, and I say, "Oh no, he's all right." I turn him on his side and start lightly slapping his face, and inside I'm still totally freaking out. But eventually he did get back up, and I played like I'd never even been worried. "You see? He's fine!"

When I got back to the door, this guy who we'd just hired was waiting for me — he was a black belt in aikido who just returned to bouncing after getting a divorce. He looked at me and said, "Dude, I have all the training in the world, but when I saw you run into that crowd of people... I mean, you could have been killed, you could have been murdered. But you just did it! I'm not made like that, I can't do that." And he quit, right then and there.

I told him right away, "It's cool, I get it," because the guy had two kids. I don't have kids, so it's easier for me to make those decisions, right? When the shit goes down like that, that kind of violence, that kind of injustice... I mean, I'm not trying to build myself up here, but even if I was just walking by on the street [and I saw someone being attacked], I'd do something.

Door Politics

A lot of people make the mistake of forgetting that we don't have to let them into a nightclub. They'll think, "It's my right to come in here," but it's not. I could not let you in for any reason at all. You could be sober and the richest person on earth, and I still don't have to let you in. It would be dumb if I didn't, but still.

[A club] isn't a public venue, it's a private place. Even if the owners are racist — not that I'd ever want to work with racist people — but if they decide I can't let people of a certain race in, or let only so many of them in, then hey, I just work there.

That movie *Knocked Up* has the most beautiful bouncer moment, where a black doorman starts talking about ratios. He says, "How do you think I feel? I'm only allowed to let 5% black people in here. That means if there's 25 people in the club, I can let in one-and-a-quarter black people. I gotta hope for a black midget in the crowd." (laughs)

But here's the deal — when any group of any color comes in male-heavy, it becomes a problem inside. Whether it's white rednecks, whether it's black people, whether it's Asians, it doesn't matter. You want a really mixed guy/girl ratio, you need that.

When I used to work at Karma, by the Toronto airport, we'd have 400 people in the lineup and my job would be to go up and down the line telling people they couldn't come in. They'd want to know why and I'd say, "Dress code. You're wearing khakis and we don't like khakis in the club," or, "We don't let those shoes in, we don't let this in, we don't let that in." So they'd go away and come back in different clothes, and we'd send 'em to the back of the line. Or we'd let them jump the line and then say, "Oh, you can't come in. You jumped the line."

Grease is the Word

So many people freak out [when we don't let them in], not realizing that we're just looking for grease [bribes]. If you're guy-heavy and you don't have anything else it takes to get past the lineup, you have to be ready to grease the doorman or else be ready to wait in line all night. But the days of doormen getting $1000 a night in Toronto are done. You'll walk away with a couple hundred in extra cash, which is great, but that's it.

The grease situation was almost always messed up. Any grease that came in would go straight to the head doorman, and he'd divvy it up. Which is so stupid, because in most cases, hardly any of that cash would make it past him.

In Vegas, there used to be a big grease system down there — one hundred, two hundred bucks a head to get in. Well, one night a guy booked bottle service at some club, but [his group] showed up guy-heavy and [the door staff] didn't let them in. The rest of the party said "Fuck this" and went somewhere else, but the original guy stayed and watched what was going down with all the grease. There must have been a lot, because I guess that head doorman drove two [Rolls Royce] Phantoms. He really wore all his money on his arm, right?

Turned out the guy who got denied worked for the IRS, and they did a huge sting on all the clubs after that. They took everything from everybody. So now, I'm sure they're still greasing but it's a different system.

Yup, the good old days are over! (laughs)

@noahdanby

@noahdanby

www.noahdanby.ca

Chapter Ten

MUHAMMED "KING MO" LAWAL

Photo courtesy Shannon Newton Photography.

"Now it's gettin' really rough, for real. Blood runnin' everywhere, and the police start runnin' in the front door."

For all his flamboyant attire and behavior, Muhammed "King Mo" Lawal rarely fails to impress when it comes time to discard the showmanship and throw down in the ring or cage.

A former NCAA Division 2 wrestling champion and Division 1 All-American, King Mo has racked up a fuck-ton of MMA victories in Japan and the USA, and earned the Strikeforce light-heavyweight world championship and the RIZIN Fighting Federation world tournament title.

Currently the King is competing in Bellator Fighting Championships, intent upon strapping yet another world championship belt around his regal waist.

Deep Ellum Live

I only bounced one time, when I was sixteen or seventeen years old in this place called Deep Ellum Live in Dallas, Texas. I got the job from an old wrestling coach who was kinda crooked, but still an okay dude. He's dead now — rest in peace, Ron.

Anyway, he was payin' me and my boys Byron and Andre five dollars an hour for five-hour shifts. I thought I was a baller, because twenty-five dollars to a kid who comes from nothin', that's good money. So we got to the place, and we were expecting it to be a hip-hop place but it's more like a rock 'n roll spot, so we didn't exactly fit in with the crowd. Plus, when I got set up out front and started checking IDs, people noticed real quick that I was looking so young, so I was always really worried about bein' busted.

One night, after we'd been working there about a month, Byron and Andre were walking around inside and I heard this commotion. I ran inside and it was crazy — I saw bottles getting broken and stuff, some blood on the floor, I thought somebody was gettin' their ass whupped! Turned out it was just a normal mosh pit, but I'd never seen a mosh pit in my life, only on TV, so I thought it was a full-blown riot!

The manager had gave Byron and Andre flashlights to signal for help by aiming it at the ceiling, and I saw Andre doing that and

King Mo reppin' one of his favorite sponsors
(Photo courtesy LanasEggWhites.com)

ran over to where he was at. Now it's gettin' really rough, for real. It was like, blood everywhere and a big melee goin', and right away the police started runnin' in the front door. Since [me, Byron and Andre are] underage, we take off, but first we run to the green room in the back and try to get our money before we go. I mean, I wanted to get outta there, but I also wanted my twenty-five dollars, you know what I'm sayin'?

We ended up getting the check for twenty-five, but since we were told when we started that we were gonna get a big check after working a few weeks, we ended up gettin' shorted for about a hundred dollars! I guess that prepared me to keep my eyes open in the pro wrestling business that I got into later, because I heard that some of the [independent wrestling] shows can be super shady, really iffy. Thank goodness I signed with a bigger organization and I didn't have to worry about that.

Man, just like my boy Andre said that night, mosh pits is some crazy, white boy stuff. You don't go in a black club and see no mosh pit! (laughs)

 *@KingMoFH*
@KingMoFH

Chapter Eleven

TARA LAROSA

Photo courtesy AlannaRalph.com

"It was time to kick everyone out and everybody was awesome —except for ONE GUY. There's ALWAYS that one freaking guy!"

On April 13, 2002, Tara LaRosa became one of fourteen history-making fighters to compete in "HOOKnSHOOT: Revolution", the first all-female mixed martial arts event ever held in North America.

Since defeating Shelby Walker on that groundbreaking show, LaRosa has gone on to rack up an impressive 22-5 record against elite-level competition. Her ultimate career landmark came in July 2007, when a ferocious battle with Kelly Kobold over the bodogFIGHT women's world championship saw LaRosa claim the most prestigious title in the pre-UFC history of women's MMA.

At the time of this writing, LaRosa still competes in a variety of combat sport organizations including the all-female Invicta FC and the iconic Pancrase Hybrid Wrestling.

The Not-So-Sophisticated Otter

My first job as a bouncer was at a place called Fat Tuesday's in Charlotte, North Carolina. I'd been doing judo for a couple of years, and little bit of jiu-jitsu and some other martial arts, and one of my buddies was managing that place and said, "Hey, you wanna do security a couple nights a week?" I said, "Sure," but then I had to ask exactly what was involved, because even then I knew that while you always hear about the "glory and glamor" of bouncing, it's never really like that. I'm not real big on street fighting, it's not my deal, so I was pretty wary but it ended up turning out okay.

I moved on from there to a place in Johnson City, Tennessee called The Sophisticated Otter. The name just screams "yuppie bar" doesn't it? (laughs) And that's exactly what it was, it was just a bunch of preppie, yuppie-type folks. It was an easy job, except on one particular night when they rented the bar out to this [musical] group called Blackout. With the hardcore fanbase that the group had, I was a little nervous. It definitely seemed like an odd mix to have that band in that bar, and I was concerned about violence. Especially with only two of us working security — me and a guy named Jeremiah — and the fact that he and one of the bartenders were the only other white people in the place.

For most of the night things went smooth, they went great. Nobody was trying to pull shit at the front door, nothing bad happened inside, everybody was awesome and just having a good time. Things were going so well that the manager left early to go to another bar he was in charge of, and left it to me and Jeremiah to wrap things up.

Last call came and went and then it was time to kick everybody out, get them to finish their drinks or turn them over. Again, everybody was awesome — except for ONE GUY. There's ALWAYS that one freaking guy! Jesus, man. This guy was hammered and really, really feelin' his oats, and he wouldn't finish or give up his drink when I asked him. It was mostly ice in it anyway, the guy was just looking to cause a scene.

Finally, Jeremiah had to try to take the drink away from him, and the guy took a swing. It popped off from there, like a chain reaction that swept from one side of the bar to the other. Suddenly, for no reason at all there's a whole bunch of people fighting! Jeremiah ended up on the bottom of a pile of three guys, and by the time I got over there, there was a huge crowd circled around them. Just a friggin' mess.

I started pulling people off, grabbing them by their shirt and dragging them off, and then some huge guy came up behind me, grabbed me and picked me up! Not a hard thing to do as I'm only five-five and a buck thirty-five, but I had a few things to say about it! (laughs) I started kicking and elbowing him, and he let go and jumped back. I think it threw him off a bit.

I grabbed another guy in a rear-naked [choke] and threw him off Jeremiah, but things were getting really bad. So I had the idea to scream *"FIVE-O! FIVE-O!"* and the crowd IMMEDIATELY scattered! One mention of the cops had them running for the exits, and that's the first time I got the idea that bouncing was more about using your brain than your fists.

Ten Car Pile-Up

I moved on from there to a place called The Lagoon in Chester, Pennsylvania, just south of Philadelphia. Now I think it's called The Deck. Good mix of people and some cool live bands — Flo Rida even came through at one point.

One thing that [the management] noticed right away was that as soon as I rolled up and started working there, the chicks were a lot less trouble. Whenever there was a problem and [the girls] saw me, they seemed to just shut up and move on. I mean, I don't particularly find myself intimidating, but I guess they did.

Even the guys seemed to be a bit easier to deal with. Guys seem to respect a female bouncer a little bit more, I guess we're not a threat to them. If you look up at a guy and say, "Look, we really need you to leave, could you do that please?" and maybe bat your eyes a little bit, a lot of them seem to be caught off guard and they comply, they go with it.

But that's not always the case. We had a problem one night when I was bouncing with a couple of buddies who I trained with at Philadelphia Fight Factory. I don't know how it started, but when it popped off and people started throwin' punches, it was all hands on deck! The scene looked like a ten-car pile up on the dance floor — nobody can move, nobody can get to the door, nobody can get to the bar, it's a fuckin' mess. Bouncers were gettin' hit, people were falling down and trippin' over each other, people who weren't even involved were gettin' hit, it was just insanity.

I ran over there with a couple of the other bouncers, and they grabbed hold of one guy. But then I saw this really big, drunk, biker-lookin' dude with a big beard and hair all over the place grabbing the shoulder of one of my buddies named McCabe. [The biker] cocked his arm back to throw a punch and I was like, "Aw, HELL, no!" Now I'm PISSED.

The guy must not have realized that I was security because he didn't even look at me twice, and I was able to get behind him and jump up on his back. I snatched him by his neck and put him in rear-naked choke, dragging him down backwards. I didn't put him out, just squeezed a little as I whispered a few choice things in his ear. Then I threw him down to the floor, and of course he looked up to see who did it. I guess I wasn't what he was expecting, because he looked like he was staring at the face of God or something! (laughs)

He got over it quick, though, and got up to grab at my buddy again. So I snatched him by his neck again, and this time I hung on and bent him over, kinda half-backward and half-sideways, and started draggin' him toward the door. This guy Chris who was working the door, he saw us comin' and he opened the door just as we got there. Then I counted 3-2-1, and fuckin' LAUNCHED this guy with every bit of energy that I had!

Larosa hunts for Katie Howard's head in Fusion Fight League.
(Photo courtesy Tara Larosa)

That was part of a game I used to play, kind of like bowling where you can't let your toes cross that line. I always used to see how far I could throw people without my feet crossing the door threshold. This time, I managed to stay inbounds while I slung the guy off my hip, and he hit the ground hard and rolled about four yards — which ended up being my best bowl yet! (laughs)

Amazon Lesbian

This story's about the first time I ever had to throw a woman out of a bar.

It was really crowded and the ladies' room was just disgusting, it was a mess. Water and soap all over the place, people been tracking through it so it's all dirty and mucked up, paper towels everywhere... women are pigs sometimes. It's disgusting.

I think there was only three stalls in the bathroom, and since I'm the only female bouncer on, one of the female bartenders comes up and asks me to check if there's something wrong in one of the stalls. And I was like, "Greeeeat." (laughs) So I wandered in there fully expecting to find the worst, like somebody passed out in the stall with puke all over the place and I'm gonna have to clean the shit up.

When I got there, I could hear people in there but the stall was locked. So I looked underneath [the door], just trying to see what was goin' on, and there was three feet [standing] in there, not just two. I thought that was a little weird. Maybe it was a person with one leg, maybe a person with three legs, I'm not sure. (laughs) So I asked, "Are you guys okay?" and I got a "Yes," so I walked back out.

About ten minutes later, somebody else came up to me and asked if I could get those same two people out of the stall. I asked what was going on in there and they just said, "I dunno, we're not even sure. Just get 'em out of there."

So I went back in and knocked on the door again, and that's when I realized what was going on — it was two ladies havin' sex! Now, this is totally new to me. Like, what are you supposed to do? I still couldn't see clearly what was happening in there — not that I was really tryin' — but they were clearly drunk and still not opening the door. I start callin' out to 'em, but I'm still bein' polite. Trying not to be an asshole until I have to be an asshole, 'cause sometimes assholes don't have the best results.

Then the female bartender who initially told me about this comes in. She goes into the next stall over, stands on the toilet, and looks over [the partition]. Right away she sees these two chicks, half-naked and goin' to town, and immediately she's like, "Get them out, just get them out!" So I start yellin' again, but still trying to be funny about it. "C'mon girls, don't make me kick down this door and drag you out by your pussy!" (laughs) And eventually, they did come out... but it was NOT pretty.

It was these two really LARGE chicks. One was kinda short and really... large. Had to be, Christ, I dunno... like, two hundred [pounds]. And the other chick was HUGE! She had wavy blond hair down to her shoulders, kind of a 1980s gym teacher sorta look, and she was well over two-fifty and every bit of six-foot-three. At that point I'm thinkin', "Oh boy, am I glad I wasn't an asshole!" (laughs)

As they walk out of the bathroom, the short girl looks really embarrassed, like, "Oh my God, we got caught." But the other one, she was not embarrassed at all. In fact, she starts mouthin' off! A few of the other bouncers hear this, and they drift over until there's four or five of us standin' there. At that point she decides she's gonna get in the face of one of our more stout bouncers — I think his name was Tom — and needless to say, he and the other guys are NOT havin' this.

Now I'm like, "Oh, Christ," because I know they want me to handle it since she's a chick. But she's also six-foot-three, so I turn to the bouncer next to me and say, "Is this my territory, or if she's over a certain height, do you guys take care of it? Is there a size restriction on this ride, or what?" (laughs)

She starts to get real heated and her hands start movin', and I can tell that Tom is about to get physical if something doesn't happen [to prevent it]. She finally made a move like she was gonna push him, and he moved forward to grab her. When I saw that, it was like, "Aw, fuck no!" because I knew that all the fun and games were over.

By now, jumpin' up on somebody's back and taking a rear-naked choke had kind of become my signature move, so I stepped on the back of her leg, climbed up and snatched her up by the neck — because no WAY can I jump that high on my own! (laughs) Then I pulled her back down to my level while Tom picked up her legs, and we kind of drug her [toward the door]. She was a heavy bitch, I tell ya. (laughs)

She starts to kickin' and wrestlin' around and she's still mouthin' off, so I was like, "Oh, I'm gonna shut your big ass up." I squeezed the choke a little bit tighter while I whispered in her ear how she could go out the front door or the back door, and if she chose the back door, people might not find her body for a few days. (laughs) That calmed her down to the point that we could get her outside and set her ass-first on the ground, and then I waved at her and said, "Have a nice night!" as we went back inside. (laughs)

We had some wild times at The Lagoon, it was a fun place.

@TaraLarosa

www.TaraLarosa.net

Chapter Twelve

TOM "THE BIG CAT" ERIKSON

Photo courtesy Tom Erikson.

"I said, 'The first guy I get my hands on is gonna get it the worst. I will get mine, but I'm gonna get one of you the worst.'"

There is simply no better word than BEAST to describe two-time NCAA Division 1 All-American and two-time Olympic wrestling team alternate Tom "The Big Cat" Erikson.

During the late 1990s, the hulking Erikson was arguably the most underrated heavyweight on the NHB/MMA scene. His debut came in 1996 at the one-night, eight-man Martial Arts Reality

Superfighting tournament, where he KOed and submitted his first two opponents en route to a grueling 40-minute time limit draw with future UFC champ Murilo Bustamante.

Seven months later, The Big Cat made an even more decisive statement in the four-man Brazil Open Fight tournament, where he won the night by bludgeoning Silvio Vieira and then sending his friend (and future UFC champion) Kevin "The Monster" Randleman out of the cage on a stretcher.

Erikson achieved further success in Japan, turning heads in Pride Fighting Championships and even the elite K-1 kickboxing organization despite an extremely basic (albeit insanely powerful) striking game.

Looking back, one simply must acknowledge Tom Erikson as one of the most athletically gifted and supremely dangerous big men in combat sports history.

The Fox

I started out [bouncing] while I was wrestling at Oklahoma State University. After I finished my eligibility at OSU, I started wrestling on the international scene — very similar to [HOOKnSHOOT Hall-of-Famer] Gary Myers, except Gary was wrestling with the army, while it was the United States freestyle team for me. I was ranked second in the US and sixth or seventh in the world, but back in those days we didn't make any money so you had to find a way to make some income.

I had a friend who owned a pretty hoppin' bar in Stillwater [Oklahoma] called The Fox. They needed bouncers, so of course I raised my hand and ended up running the security staff. The great thing about that job was that some of the other bouncers were wrestlers too, so we had a nice bond where we knew that we had each other's backs.

[UFC Hall-of-Famer] Don [Frye] actually bounced at a place called Eskimo Joe's, about fifty yards down the street from The Fox. Man, I remember going into Joe's and seeing Don do some of his work! (laughs)

MAULER'S NOTE: Check out Don "The Predator" Frye and "Iron Bear" Gary Myers' chapters in When We Were Bouncers *Vol. 1 for the gory details of what those animals got up to*

I was actually relatively afraid of going out in Oklahoma. I was from the south side of Chicago where, if they have a reason, they're probably gonna shoot you, club you and leave you in an alley. But down in Oklahoma, they don't need a reason — they fight for pride. A little 'ol cowboy will come up and wanna fight you just to prove how tough he is and impress his girlfriend and his buddies. That randomness was actually more scary to me than the hardcore criminals of Chicago. Of course, the good side is that in Oklahoma, a couple of hours after you fought a guy you could be having a beer with him! (laughs)

Dumpster Douchebag

Friday and Saturday nights [at The Fox] were crazy. The university had a pretty good football team — Barry Sanders and Thurman Thomas were down there, they had some pretty studly players. If it was a game night and the players were coming back with a big win, they'd be hitting it hard and things would get pretty rowdy. My bosses were very, very football-friendly in terms of taking care of those guys — buying 'em drinks, pitchers, whatever. But the players generally knew not to take too many liberties.

One night this regular guy, not a football player, is just goin' crazy, and I signal a couple of the other bouncers to get 'im outta there. They throw him out with no trouble, but a half-hour later I see the same guy standing in a corner! I don't know how he got past the guys at the door, but this time I escort the guy out myself and tell him, "Look, you can't come back in. You're drunk, you gotta go." I'm still being cordial, not putting my hands on him or anything, because I don't like to initially touch someone. That just takes things to another level.

So I escort him out and sure enough, he ends up back in the bar AGAIN and he's even drunker this time! He sees me and starts trying to dart through the crowd, but I chase him down, grab him, and pin him to the ground. I'm like, "That's it — you're out!" But while he's laying there he twists around sideways, grabs my shirt, and rips the hell out of it right down the front!

Now I'm furious. I put him in a little arm bar to turn him over face down. Then I reach down and grab a good handful of his jeans — and whatever else is in his crotch area — and [with the other hand I grab] the back of his neck. Then I pick him up like a sack of potatoes and start marching toward the exit. Since my hands are both full, I'm cutting through the crowd by bumping his head into people to clear them out of the way. (laughs) I don't have to do that too much though, because once I bump a few people, they see what's goin' on and they start movin'. I'm taking the guy toward a side entrance that's got one of those safety bars that you push to go out, and since my hands are full and I'm angry, I just use his head to open the door. (laughs) It wasn't that bad, though — he wasn't bleedin' and I didn't crush his skull or anything.

Erikson clashes with future UFC champ Fabricio Werdum in Japan's Pride Fighting Championships (Photo courtesy Susumu Nagao)

We get outside and I'm about to just chuck 'im, but I'm really pissed because my shirt's all shredded and I can feel that he scratched me on the neck. So when I see a dumpster across the street, I think, "I'm gonna get this motherfucker." I carry the guy all the way across the street, hoist him up, and throw him into the dumpster. Then I tell him that if he comes back again, it's gonna be a lot worse.

We didn't see him again after that. (laughs)

Gridiron Gorillas

The guys who owned The Fox were pretty industrious guys, and eventually they bought a club down in Norman [Oklahoma] and called it The Fox as well. The University of Oklahoma was down there and their football team was on fire, I believe they played Penn State for the national title that year. Barry Switzer was running things and they had Keith Jackson, Brian Bosworth, Jamelle Holieway, Charles Thompson... they had a whole crew down there. Needless to say, that town REALLY catered to their football players.

It wasn't long before the new Fox was doing really well, but it also had a problem with the football players kinda taking over the place. Bossing people around and such. It was becoming a little bit of an issue, and one of the owners started saying to them, "Hey, I've got a guy up in Stillwater who will take care of you guys. You don't calm down, I'm gonna bring him down here." But the players were cocky, they were like, "Yeah, right! You're not bringing anybody here who we can't handle."

So the owner eventually did have me come down there. At first [it was] just to take a night off and have a good time while he showed off his big, bad wrestler. I met the football players and they were actually really good guys, but they were also... I don't wanna say "bullies." They were just knocking guys around and being very self-confident in a bad sort of way, you know? When they got rowdy I would joke around with 'em, saying, "You guys are lucky I don't work here." But they weren't believing it. "So what if you did? What are you gonna do?" I just smiled and told 'em, "You'll see if they ever bring me down here. You'll find out." After the bar closed that night, we went to some party and I ended up hanging out with a guy named Mark Hutson, a two-time All-American offensive lineman. Big ol' dude, and a good guy, too. Had a great time.

But a couple of weeks later, the boss called me up and said, "Come on out. The guys are still being assholes and I need you to set the tone." So I got my work shirt and headed down there. When the players rolled in that night, they said, "You're not drinking with us?" and I said, "No, tonight I'm working. I gotta babysit you assholes." Once again they all laughed, saying, "What are you gonna do?"

They congregated around a pool table at the back of the bar, and it didn't take long before they were a problem. Knocked one of our waitresses over and spilled her drinks all over the place. That came out of the waitress's pay so of course she was a little upset, and the boss said to me, "You gotta go talk to those guys." I went back there to tell 'em to knock it off, and as always, they weren't hearin' it.

So I said, "I'll tell you what. There's a whole bunch of you guys, and together you can definitely kick my ass. That's a given. But here's the thing — one of you is gonna get his ass kicked twice as bad as I get it. The first guy I get my hands on is the guy who's gonna get it the worst. I can make that promise, I will get mine but I'm gonna get one of you the worst." But they still laughed it off. After all, it was just me against ten of them.

About an hour later, they pulled some more shit and that was it. I went back over there and said, "Enough. Somebody's gotta go." Now, I'm old-school, so I was already sighting on the biggest and baddest dude in the group. If you've been around the block, you know that if you take out the big dog in any group, the rest will all lay down... in theory, anyway. (laughs)

In this case, the biggest, baddest dude was Mark Hutson, the guy I'd been drinking with the last time I was in there. He was drunk and out of control, just acting ridiculously stupid, and I tapped him on the shoulder and said, "You gotta go." All his boys started chirping in his ear about how he wasn't going anywhere, how I couldn't do a thing. But I could, and I did. I took Hutson's arm — one hand on his wrist and the other on his shoulder — and started turning him toward the door. He yanked himself away and squared up like he was gonna hit me, and everybody was like, "UH oh" as if it was the gunfight at the OK Corral.

Hutson clenched his fist and threw this big ol' haymaker of a right, but I saw it coming and did a level change, ducking underneath it while throwing a right of my own. I wasn't trying to punch him, just trying to get my arm up around his neck as his punch went over my head. Then I came up with my head behind his shoulder and my arm on his neck, jumping up onto the side of his body and wrapping my legs around him. [The grip I had was] almost like a rear-naked choke but on the side, and I locked my hands together and clamped down TIGHT, riding him all the way to the floor. He dropped to a knee but I wasn't lettin' go, I was determined to choke him all the way out. He eventually passed out and collapsed, and everybody who was watching was losing it. Back then most people weren't familiar with chokes, so they all thought that I killed 'im!

After I eventually let go, I put Hutson on his back, planted my knee in his chest and started slapping him in the face, "Wake up! Wake up!" When he opened his eyes, I said, "I told you! I told you sonsabitches what I was gonna do, but you didn't listen! Now, you do it again and I'm gonna drag your ass right outta here!"

After that, the problem was over and we were the best of friends from then on! (laughs) In fact, I created about twenty new bouncers that night, because after watching me choke out one of their big, bad dudes right in front of 'em, they all knew the ass-beating they were gonna get if I REALLY got pissed off.

Grabbing a Predator by the Tail

This ain't a bouncing story, it happened at a wrestling meet, but since I mentioned Don Frye before, I'm gonna tell it. You can check this out with him if you want, he'll confirm it.

I was coaching Don in a Bedlam Match against University of Oklahoma. Oklahoma State vs. University of Oklahoma is a huge rivalry. We HATED those guys — F 'em, we hated 'em.

> *MAULER'S NOTE: Any football, basketball or wrestling match between Oklahoma State and the University of Oklahoma is considered to be a part of the very appropriately-named "Bedlam Series"*

Now, Don was an undersized heavyweight, only about two-twenty-five. Still a bad little dude, though. Not a world-beater, but a very good, above-average wrestler. He was up against this guy named Carl Presley, who was actually from Illinois.

Presley was just a young pup, and he started gettin' dirty with Don. They both started pushin' and shovin', kinda whackin' each other, and the referee kept giving 'em warnings. Then they got in another flurry, and all of a sudden it went from being a wrestling match to a full-on street fight! They were teeing off on each other, just SWINGING! Don had a temper, man, and he was trying to take Presley's head OFF.

I jumped off the bench, ran onto the mat, and grabbed Don with one arm around his waist. Then I snatched him up off the ground and pinned him to my hip like a mother carrying a baby! (laughs) Presley was still going crazy, so I put my other hand in his chest and stiff-armed him away, screaming, *"KNOCK IT OFF! KNOCK IT OFF!"*

Surprisingly enough, after things had settled down a bit, nobody got kicked off the mat. I think the people were so in shock at what happened that they didn't know what to do. The match just continued and nobody even got dinged a point — no team points, no nothin'! (laughs)

I still know the referee from that match, and to this day I joke around with him about how I had to jump off the bench and save his life. Man, that was crazy!

🐦 *@TomErikson2*

Chapter Thirteen

JOE R. LANSDALE

Photo courtesy Karen Lansdale.

"The judge looked at me and then looked at my boss, who had a black eye from where I'd driven his plastic glasses into his skull."

One of the most talented and prolific authors of our time, "Champion Mojo Storyteller" Joe R. Lansdale has over forty novels and a mountain of short stories to his credit. A winner of the Edgar Award, eight Bram Stoker Awards and too many other honors and accolades to list here, Lansdale has seen his work adapted to the big and small screens multiple times, including the brilliant and hilarious *Bubba Ho-Tep* starring Bruce Campbell and Ossie Davis, the intense *Cold in July* starring Don Johnson, Sam Shepard and Michael C. Hall, and the truly unique *Hap and Leonard* TV series which enters its second season as this book goes to print.

Outside of the literary realm, Lansdale is also a member of the International Martial Arts Hall of Fame and the creator/Senior Grand Master of the Shen Chuan: Martial Science martial arts system.

Training with Dad

Everybody where I grew up fought. I started wrestling and boxing when I was eleven, and then went into judo, kempo, hapkido, Thai boxing, and taekwondo. This was back when taekwondo was not a sport like it is now, it was a real martial art. I picked a lot of [my martial arts training] up from my father. He was forty-two when I was born, and he was my first instructor. During the Great Depression he was a boxer and carnival wrestler — a "shooter" — so he taught me boxing, wrestling, and some jiu-jitsu that he had picked up. He was an old country boy, and he called it *joo-jitsey*. "That's a *joo-jitsey* trick there, y'do that an' you'll break his goddamn arm!" (laughs) That's how he used to teach, I loved it. All the stuff you see in Brazilian jiu-jitsu today, he showed me back then.

I even did bare-knuckle [fighting] for a while because my father had, and I wanted to see if I could do it. It hurts! We'd get a few people together and it would be like mixed martial arts before there was mixed martial arts. We used everything we knew — judo, wrestling, boxing, all that stuff. Hardly any rules, we didn't even match size. I think it was that you couldn't bite or poke an eye, and you could only kick lightly to the groin. Which I think's a funny thing, "lightly." (laughs) And we were doing that for nothing, we were doing it for fun! People were always banged up and hurt, but we enjoyed it.

One Against Many

I became a bouncer by being a manager for a band, a rock 'n roll band called The First State Bank out of Gladewater, Texas. I was their combination manager, roadie and bouncer. I was only seventeen.

At that time, people weren't allowed to bring drinks in [to the shows], but some people came in drunk or brought liquor with 'em, and they were usually the troublemakers. I learned pretty quick to tell who they were, and most of the time I could just ask 'em to leave and they'd do it. They'd be a little fussy, but they'd go out begrudgingly. But one night, I made the mistake of going outside with a group of four guys, and I learned that you don't do that.

Fortunately for me, one of 'em was scared and the rest of 'em were glad of it. The [scared] guy panicked and tried to choke me. He didn't try anything clever because I don't think he knew anything clever, he just pushed me up against the wall with this goofy, straight-armed choke like The Mummy or The Frankenstein Monster, that kind of thing. Of course, I had learned all kinds of things in martial arts for that, and I'd been in a lot of fights already. But a lot of techniques such as beatin' the arms down, or beatin' your way inside, they just don't work if you're pinned and a guy's strong. Not unless you're stronger than him, or you catch him just right.

So he was holding me against the wall, and without thinking I put the palm of my hand close to one of his hands, right where the wrist bends. Then turned my shoulders, and his hands popped right off, easy as pie. After that, I hit him, armlocked him, and threw him down on the ground, and the other guys didn't do anything.

That wasn't the most exciting thing that ever happened to me, but it was one of the most valuable in a pure self-defense situation because I discovered a technique that works so well, I still teach it. And it came about purely through accident.

Putting It All Together

It seemed like there was a fight every other week, because at that high school age everyone had testosterone, everybody who had dates was provin', and it all helped me to develop what I learned to do. I found that what worked, even if the guys were bigger than me — which was frequently the case because I'm about five-ten — was to get right on top of 'em no matter how big they were, swat their arm away, and get to the side. I always did better by swarming 'em in such a way that I got to the outside so I could hit 'em in the kidneys. For me, all those early fights were lessons learned.

One night, I got jumped in the parking lot by several guys and hit in the head with a tire tool. I ducked and it just clipped the top of my head, and then I got my back against a car and whipped every one of 'em for a while. I was fortunate they weren't swarmin' me because they were all scared. A lot of times, if they all swarm you at once, you're pretty well screwed. One of 'em would come at me and I'd knock him down, then another guy would come at me and I'd knock *him* down. But somewhere along the line, one of 'em finally did get up and hit me, and next thing I knew, I woke up in the parking lot! (laughs) I guess those guys could have finished me off right there if they'd have been crazy, but thankfully they just left. Even though that didn't end so well, I learned that if I got my back up against a car, I was able to do better [against multiple opponents].

I don't wanna sound like this is a brag on fighting or anything, because I don't think that's smart. At the same time, I think that you do learn from what you've [experienced], and when I teach martial arts, I teach from the standpoint of actually having been hit. I know what it feels like to be hit, and know what kind of techniques I've tried to use that did not work, at least for me. You develop from reality, and for me that's a big part of martial arts — learning from your mistakes as well as your successes.

Dairy Queen and Treasure City

I had one situation in Longview, Texas, in the parking lot of a place called Treasure City that sold all sorts of stuff, clothes and things like that. It was like an early Wal-Mart that did not catch on. I had a Bears sticker on the back of my car — that was the name of our high school football team — and three guys saw it and they weren't gonna give me any quarter. I remember telling 'em, "Hey, it's just a Bears sticker!" But these guys were from another school and they were determined to fight.

That's how foolish these things were, growin' up in East Texas in these little, rough towns. I think people looked for entertainment [through violence] because there wasn't anything else. They'd see someone from out of town and say, "They're from Gladewater, we're from Longview — they're our foes." I remember when I was young, they had a big gang fight at the Dairy Queen in Gladewater. People got broken arms and legs, a guy even got his eye put out with a bottle thrown at 'im. And the whole thing was over, "We're from Pinetree, you're from Gladewater." That's stupid. It's nothing more than territorial bullshit.

Anyway, once I realized that these boys were set to fight, I rushed the one closest to me. All this talk about, "You pick the biggest one [or] you pick the one that's mouthin'," all that's bullshit. I learned from previous situations that the first thing you do is you swarm the guy closest to you. The other two did come in, but I was able to keep the first guy between me and them. I got behind him and was holdin' onto the back of his collar, hittin' him in the ribs with every shot I could get. When he finally started gettin' weak in the knees, I threw him down and got the other one closest to me while the third one ran. The big thing is to hit repeatedly, keep hittin', and hit the one closest to you. Don't try to use any philosophy like "Hit the one that's talkin'" because sometimes that guy will let his friends do the fightin', while other times he's the fighter. It varies from situation to situation.

I saw this movie where Tom Cruise was tellin' these guys what they were all gonna do and how they were all gonna act, and well, it's a crock of shit. I've been in every situation possible, and none of that kinda shit works because you don't know that individual person's reasons or philosophy. You can take certain things and say that they work more frequently than others, but this idea that you know what everybody's going to do [is bullshit]. Now, I think some confidence does help, it can cause some hesitation, but the only thing that [consistently] causes hesitation is just beatin' the Pure-D dogshit out of the first one closest to you. Takin' him down and givin' him everything you got. Because then, people go, "That happened to him, that could happen to me."

Take This Job... And This Punch Inna Face

There was a guy I worked for in construction in Tyler [Texas]. I think it was about '73, the year [my wife] Karen and I got married. He was also a preacher — and you know, you should always be suspect of them (laughs) — and he would just jack with me every day. I had long hair, and he just would not quit. "Hey, baby," and stuff like that. He was a big guy — lean, tall, big — and at that time I was twenty-one and only about 148 pounds.

One day we had a bunch of doors that we were supposed to stack, so me and this other guy got 'em stacked up above our heads. Then I went to the boss and said, "Scuse me, we got these doors stacked, where would you like us to start another stack?" He says, "Stack on top of [the original pile]," and I said, "Well, that's higher that we can reach. What would you suggest?" And he... I don't remember what he said after that, but he got mad and grabbed my blue jean jacket with his left hand. And when he did, I just speed-hit 'im — POP-POP-POP. He went down, and then he went to the hospital with some internal injuries.

I just went home, but the Sheriff's Department came and got me. The officer who came out to our house was a guy I knew, and he said, "Man, you gotta go in, but a lot of people saw it happen so I think it's gonna be okay." So I went [to court], and the judge looked at me and then looked at [my boss], who had a black eye from where I'd driven his plastic glasses into his skull. The judge got him to admit that he'd grabbed me first, and then said, "Wait a minute... you picked on THIS little guy?" (laughs) I always found that funny, that he was all lumped up and I didn't have a mark on me but I got off because of my size!

Dealing with She-Devils

I only have one bad story about having to throw women out of a place. Man, they are like tigers! It's because they don't have any ego the way that men do. Men's ego makes them hesitate because they think, "What if I look bad?" Women don't have that. They have a kind of absolute abandon, and their lack of technique becomes technique. Clawin', bitin', kickin', swingin', and just as rapid as they can. There's also the built-in hesitation [from males] because we're taught, "You don't hit a woman, you just don't do that," which can make things even more deadly.

I only had that one time, breakin' up a fight between two women at a dance, pulling the top girl off the bottom one. I guess I hesitated because I didn't want to hurt 'em, and as I was pulling the top girl off, I got hit in the head about five times by the other one! She's trying to hit the girl I'm holding, and I got caught between 'em. I finally reached out, caught the arm of the girl who was hittin' me, and wristlocked her. Bent her wrist down and got her to stop. Now, even doing just that made me feel like a big bully — but you know what? That was immature thinking. Because it don't matter who somebody is, they can hurt you just as good as the other person. Male, female, little, big... doesn't matter.

I've seen that sort of thing happen with other [guys] that were bouncin', and it was usually kinda funny in a way because they didn't know what to do, either. I think it's the psychological, cultural aspect of [men being physical with women], tied with the fact that women are just absolutely ruthless fighters when they finally reach that point.

No Matter How Good You Are...

I never want this to sound like it's great to go out and do these things. I'm just tellin' you from experience that they happened, right or wrong. One time, one of my students came to me to ask if he should take a job bouncing at a certain club, and I said, "I don't think you should. That club is just one of those really bad places. You're gonna end up gettin' hurt or hurtin' somebody." And he ended up hurtin' somebody really, really bad. I had done that myself, I knew how it felt, and it messed [my student] up pretty bad.

Another one of my students had someone pull a knife on him. Now, to me, there is no really good gun or knife defense except to run like hell. If they're close and you can't run, your only choice is to take that [gun or knife] away, which is what my student did, but the odds are not on your side.

[As far as fighting goes] I'm good, I'm fuckin' good, I'm just gonna say it. I'm in my sixties, but even though I'm on my downside I can whip somebody's ass that would never expect it. But you know what? I can also have a bad day. I could have my mind on something else, or I could come across a guy who's ten times better than me, or a guy who doesn't know shit but he just gets me first. Any kinda fight, no matter what you know, can go the other way. Once you really realize how much is based on slick shoes, bad terrain, if you're feeling ill, if you're surprised, if a guy can sneak up on you... no matter how good you are, you can be defeated.

A lot of the people you fight on the street aren't trained fighters but they have no respect for themselves, and that makes them some of the deadliest and most unpredictable opponents that you can encounter.

🐦 *@joelansdale*

🌐 *www.joerlansdale.com*

Chapter Fourteen

RICHARD NORTON

Photo courtesy Adrian Carr.

*"I used to screen Stevie Nicks' mail, and one day
I found a telegram from some dude
saying that he was going to kill her."*

While the word "legend" has become so overused that it has almost lost its meaning, it is in its truest sense applicable to actor, stuntman, director, producer, stunt/fight coordinator, celebrity bodyguard, and martial arts icon Richard Norton.

During the late 1970s, Norton made his way out of his native Australia to forge a career in the film and TV industry, starting with his big-screen debut in Chuck Norris' cult classic *The Octagon*.

During the years since then, he has battled against and teamed up with a laundry list of cinematic martial arts mainstays such as Jackie Chan, Cynthia Rothrock, Sammo Hung, Benny Urquidez and David Carradine, all while accumulating black belts and accolades in various fighting disciplines including Brazilian jiu-jitsu, Chun Kuk Do, Gojo-ryu karate, Uquidokan kickboxing, and the Zen Do Kai freestyle fighting system that Norton co-created over 40 years ago.

Norton's work can be seen in many big-budget action epics including *Mad Max: Fury Road, Suicide Squad,* and *Ghost in the Shell,* and he can also be spotted on the Starz series *Spartacus: War of the Damned* sporting a sixtysomething physique that would put most twentysomethings to shame.

But prior to his beyond-prestigious film career, Norton's bread and butter was bodyguarding some of the most famous rock 'n roll acts on Planet Earth.

Starting Up

I always saw my job on the road as being much like a babysitter as well as a bodyguard. The common perception of a bouncer or bodyguard is that you're just a big meathead who can't wait to bang heads together, but people need to understand that in my experience, [a bodyguard's] purpose was quite often to be a friend and a confidante. So many of the fond memories of that period of my life certainly aren't about the violence. Of course, I was there and able to handle it in case that sort of thing should come about, but more times than not, it was about that friendship as much as the security that I was there to give the artists.

I got into bodyguarding through one of my oldest friends and mentors, Bob Jones, who I was partners with in a string of martial arts schools called Zen Do Kai. At one point, we had about 500 schools throughout Australia. Bob is the one who got me started as a doorman, or bouncer, in pubs and discotheques as a teenager. Later, we did security at some rock concerts through an Australian entrepreneur named Paul Dainty — we even did the Australian version of Woodstock. Whenever Paul brought out a big rock'n roll act, he'd give Bob and I a call.

I think that we were successful in this line of work not just because we could do the job, but because we also didn't look anything like typical bodyguards. Meaning that so often the type of bands we worked with wanted a security presence around them, but liked their bodyguards to be low key, to look like we could even be members of the band and to just be there in case a situation arose.

The Rolling Stones

My real introduction to the world of rock 'n roll bodyguard work came in 1973 with The Rolling Stones' tour of Australia. Working with the band ended up involving more than just keeping the guys safe, as I also ended up sometimes acting as a fitness trainer and martial arts instructor. Mick [Jagger], as anyone who has watched him onstage would realize, was well aware of the need to stay incredibly fit, so he loved the idea of doing some martial arts with me. I would quite often end up teaching him some basic [techniques] in his hotel at some ungodly time like four in the morning, because [the band] would often get so wired and amped up after a show that nobody wanted to go to bed.

I'd find myself in the funniest situations with those guys. One time in Adelaide after a show, they had chairs set up with long boards borrowed from some construction site, going between their adjoining rooms with all these local strippers doing a parade along the planks from one room to the other! Ah, such were the perks of rock 'n roll. (laughs)

One of my jobs was to sometimes rustle people up for the after parties in the band members' suites at the hotel. We would scour the bars and lobbies of whatever hotels we were in, and offer invites to all the lovelies we could find. Of course, a lot of the girls we invited had husbands and boyfriends with them at the time, so once the elevator reached the band's floor, it was our job to break the news to the guys in tow that, "Sorry, it's ladies only." The funny part — or tragic part, depending on your point of view — was how many of those "ladies" just kept walking, while we shoved their men back into the elevator and sent them back down to the ground! (laughs)

One night, a group of very well-dressed ladies and men who were in town for a flower convention turned up at the band's floor. They'd obviously had a lot to drink, and they had heard that The Stones were in the hotel and wanted to get out on the band's floor to maybe meet them. We greeted them with, "I'm sorry, this floor's closed to the general public," [which ended] up with one rather large fellow deciding he wasn't going to be told what to do, and becoming very aggressive and belligerent. So my fellow bodyguard at the time, a guy named Stewie, "gently" punched him in the eye and sent him flying back into the elevator with the doors closing behind him.

A couple of seconds later, as the elevator started to descend, the thing jammed due to this gentleman throwing his weight around inside. Now, this was probably around midnight, and by four the next morning, here they were, still in there. Judging from the sounds coming through the door, the guy Stewie had punched was losing it, and all the other people with him were quite desperate, too. Well, this became like our entertainment for the night (laughs), with us and the whole band just lounging around the passageway outside the elevator, waiting for the hotel repairman to arrive.

Finally, after much moaning and drama from the occupants, Keith Richards went over to the elevator door. Acting like he was the elevator repairman, he said, "Listen everybody, this is very important! I need all of you to move very close to the door so you can hear this. This is urgent, so come to the door and listen very carefully." We heard all this shuffling and bit of moaning and groaning as everyone came close, and then it all got very quiet again before Keith finally said, "I just want to let you know... we're all going to bed now." (laughs) Oh, man, it was just pandemonium after that!

When the doors finally opened, everyone charged out wanting to murder us all. But Mick and the boys signed autographs for everybody, gave them all headshots and defused the whole thing, with everyone going home happy.

Famous Fitness

After that, I went on to work with Bob [Jones] for quite a number of acts. Joe Cocker, Fleetwood Mac, Stevie Nicks when she went solo, David Bowie for six years, Linda Ronstadt, and James Taylor for around 14 years. And one of my favorites, the Swedish pop sensation ABBA, who by the way were such wonderful people to be around. One of my dubious "jobs" was to work the girls [of the band] out nearly every day, often on local beaches or poolside, with the beautiful Anna and Frieda clad only in tiny bikinis. Hey, it's a dirty job but somebody has to do it! (laughs)

Richard somehow enduring the task of training ABBA's scantily-attired
Anna Fältskog (Photo courtesy Richard Norton)

This again is what a lot of the bands liked from me, that as an aside from being their security I would get them up in the mornings — at least, those that I could — give them good fitness workouts and try to get 'em fit, at least for their time on the road. In fact, Rolling Stone magazine ended up doing an article on me, because they were quite intrigued with hearing stories about these rock 'n roll bands going out on the road and coming back in better shape than when they left! I mean, that was almost unheard of back then.

David Bowie

When I first met David Bowie, he challenged me to a one-armed pushup contest. There we were, banging off one-armed pushups in the middle of a restaurant! (laughs) David was great. He taught me that this perception that people often have [of celebrities] is so off-base [compared] to the real personality of the artist. Like with actors, [rock musicians] will often role-play a persona that they choose to put out there for public consumption. One time at a concert, David said, "Look at all those kids out there in the audience. They're dressed the same way I was on my last tour, but they'll never catch me looking the same again." He was such a chameleon, all about continually changing and reinventing himself. Offstage, I found him to be so incredibly articulate and intelligent, the perfect English gentleman. He really was just so different from what anyone would perceive the David Bowie of that era to be.

L to R: Producer Hugh Padgham, Richard, and the late, great David Bowie
(Photo courtesy Richard Norton)

Colossal Cocker-Up

Then you had Joe Cocker, a guy who had a heart of gold and one of the best voices in the business. Man, could he sing! Funnily — to me at least — he had some of his best shows after he'd had a shitload to drink. That whole thing he used to do with his hands [while performing], that was all very real, and totally exacerbated after many fine lagers. (laughs) I've got so many funny stories about that guy.

One night, we were in Sydney at one of those "Les Girls" type of clubs, and he invited this lovely young lass back to the hotel. So here we were sitting in Joe's room and he was on the floor with this girl, pashing on [kissing] until about three in the morning. Finally, I felt compelled to whisper, "Um, Joe... that's really a *guy*." (laughs) He just looked up at me, obviously not wanting to hear what I had just said, and went, *"Noooo"* and kept pashing on. But around half an hour later, the kicker comes when this blonde "lady" finally looks at Joe intently, and in a voice deeper than mine, says, "You know, Joe — I really *am* a man." Well, Joe just freaked out and disappeared for the rest of the night, leaving us rolling around on the floor in fits of laughter! He [always swore] that he just passed out that night, and that none of it really happened. Too bloody funny.

Stevie and Joe

I was also out on the road as personal bodyguard with Stevie Nicks for a number of years. One of my most tense nights with her was when she was playing in Oklahoma. We pulled up outside the venue, and all I remember hearing as I am getting out of the limo is someone announcing over the loudspeakers, "Everybody please leave your guns and knives in the car, don't bring them into the auditorium!" (laughs) For fuck's sake! Welcome to America.

At one particular show with Stevie, it was festival seating where there are no assigned seats, and everyone ends up just standing and jostling to get as close to the stage as possible. I'm looking down at thousands of people cramming against the barricade, and very early in the show I start noticing as many as a dozen kids passing out and getting carried away by the staff. So when Stevie came offstage for her first costume change, I quickly said, "Stevie, this is really serious. There are kids getting hurt out there." Now, don't get me wrong, Stevie is such a caring person and sincerely loves her fans, but I don't think at this moment she fully understood how bad the situation had gotten. So she just went back out again and went on singing.

Out of concern and desperation, I located the promoter and said, "Look, you need to stop this, as this is serious." When he failed to heed my warning, I took the step of saying to him, "If you don't do something right now, I am going to drag Stevie off the stage!" He of course freaked, because [stopping a show] is a very dangerous thing to do with big crowds. I mean, you run the risk of having the whole crowd turn on you, because a lot of the people behind those at the front obviously don't understand, and they don't react kindly to their concert being interrupted. Anyway, he wouldn't do it, so I took the decision of going out there and literally dragging Stevie off the stage, made her understand how many kids were really getting hurt. She was so distraught when she finally realized the situation.

Joe Walsh was the opening act on this tour and a good friend, so I appealed to him and said, "Joe, please, I need your help here with the crowd." Joe's got such an amiable way about him, and fortunately the punters [fans] loved him, so he got to the mic and appealed to the crowd. "Please, you've got to take some steps back. People up front here are getting seriously hurt." By the grace of God, it all worked out — the crowd didn't kick up a big fuss and they moved back, with the concert going on and leaving most everyone happy.

It's those sorts of things that people often don't appreciate are part of our job — looking after the client for sure, but also looking out for the audience and all the punters out there in the crowd.

Psycho Stalker

I used to [screen] a lot of Stevie's mail, and one day I found a telegram from some dude saying that he was basically going to kill her at a particular venue, which he actually named! I believe her next show was in Florida or somewhere like that. We ended up with the FBI being present in numbers, because that same guy had sent a similar threatening telegram to then-President Ronald Reagan. [The stalker] even sent his name, address and photograph with those threats, which tells you that this is a totally irrational and wacko person. The anonymous threats you don't really worry about as much, but when someone is that loony that they are willing to include all their personal details along with the threat, that's cause for particular alarm. Well, it turned out to be a good thing that the FBI were there, because amazingly enough, this crazy dude did in fact end up being in the second row of Stevie's show! Thankfully the FBI guys spotted him, and safely and efficiently got him out of there right away.

Wolf in Sheep's Clothing

A similar incident happened with Linda Ronstadt. I was outside her dressing room door, and this little guy turned up wearing a black suit and a bowler hat, and carrying a briefcase. He wasn't wearing a backstage pass as was always required, so I stopped him and said, "Excuse me, who are you? You shouldn't be back here." He quite confidently said to me, "Oh, I'm Miss Ronstadt's physician. She's called for me." I replied that I didn't think so, but out of courtesy I had a local security guard stand with the guy whilst I went inside and asked Linda if she'd called for a doctor. She predictably said no, as she would normally do something like that through me anyway. So I went back out and told the security guard to walk the little guy right out of the arena.

About an hour later I bumped into that same security guard, and he remarked about how strange the little guy was. When I asked why he thought that, [the guard] told me that as he was walking [the little guy] off the premises, the man suddenly stopped and asked him, "Would you like to see what's in my briefcase?" Then he'd opened it up, and lo and behold, there sitting in the briefcase was a big carving knife! This guy had gotten

Richard with Linda Ronstadt
(Photo courtesy Richard Norton)

through a police line, past all the local security, made his way literally to Linda's door purely because he was a little, unassuming guy who looked the part of a doctor. That just illustrated to me what this job is all about — you really are that last line of defense, and there for that one-in-a-million chance that it all goes horribly wrong.

Remember, it only takes that one potential threat to succeed, and it's all over.

James Taylor Overhears History

When I was working for James Taylor, people would sometimes ask me, "Why does James need a bodyguard? We all love him!" To which I would often respond, "Most everybody loved John Lennon, too. So why is he dead?" People keep thinking of the normal, rational person in these cases, but again, my job is to be on guard for that one-in-a-

Richard with "Sweet Baby James"
(Photo courtesy Richard Norton)

million punter who has his or her own twisted agenda, and will go to any lengths to succeed in destroying a celebrity's life.

On that note, I remember one day in 1980 [when I was] in Peter Asher's office. Peter was a mega-manager, and at that time he managed both Linda Ronstadt and James Taylor. Peter had been a part of "Peter and Gordon", a hugely famous English duo around the Beatles' day, and at one time Peter's sister was engaged to Paul McCartney.

Anyway, on this day I remember Peter being on the phone with James, who was calling from his apartment on Central Park West. So Peter finishes the call and hangs up, then turns to me and says, "Gosh, that's weird. James said he just heard a noise that sounded like a gunshot." Well, we would later find out that what James had heard was in fact the gunshot that killed John Lennon! What's really bizarre is that only one hour before, [Lennon's killer Mark David] Chapman had approached James on the street and gotten an autograph from him. But obviously, Chapman had John Lennon in his mind, and that was who got it.

John Belushi

One night, Linda [Ronstadt] was doing Saturday Night Live in New York. I was hanging out backstage with her, giving her some light exercises and stretching her out the way I often did before a performance, when John Belushi came in. From that little meeting, I was suddenly the only person that John wanted as his bodyguard, and for no other reason than because he was such good friends with Linda. I guess me being okay with her made me okay with him. That, by the way, is kind of how that industry worked. You didn't get a gig like mine by sending in a resume and headshot, you got it by word of mouth from a friend, manager or artist that gave you a reputation as someone who could be trusted and depended on.

A huge thrill for me is that as result of that meeting, I ended up working for John during the filming of the famous Blues Brothers movie. I mean, I got to meet John Landis, Ray Charles, Aretha Franklin and all these other incredible artists. When the movie wrapped and it came time for Belushi to do the Blues Brothers tour with Dan Aykroyd, I was unavailable because of commitments to other bands, but John actually said that he was not going to do it unless I came with him! Pretty crazy stuff, huh? In the end, I set John up with a close friend and fellow martial artist, Bill 'Superfoot' Wallace.

Bill tragically would end up being the one who found John after he died [of a drug overdose] at the famous Chateau Marmont Hotel on the Sunset Strip in Los Angeles. James Taylor and I were on tour when it happened, and we ended up flying in a private jet to Martha's Vineyard for Belushi's funeral. Various famous musicians and a lot of the cast from Saturday Night Live were there. What an incredibly sad occasion that was.

The Greatest Compliment

Recently, James [Taylor] came to Australia to play some shows, and he flew my wife Judy and I up to Sydney to see him and to meet [Taylor's collaborator] Carole King. The nicest thing about that visit for me personally was when James introduced me to Carole backstage and said, "You know, Richard actually helped change my life." Wow. This was in part because of the fact that when I first started working with James, he was into quite a few habits that weren't necessarily conducive to good health — I shall say no more on that. But as a result of our daily workouts and martial arts training on the road, exercise suddenly became James' addiction. At the time I caught up with James in Australia, it had been over twenty-five years since he had even touched alcohol. I can't tell you how good that made me feel, to have had such a personal impact on the life of someone I worked with and respected so much.

From Sold-Out Arenas to Movie Sets

I was actually blessed to have had that relationship with a lot of the people I toured with back in the day, it was a really wonderful time in my life. Working with the bands is what eventually led me into the world of movies, as I first ended up in the US after being offered full time employment here with Linda Ronstadt. My partner Bob Jones had earlier brought Chuck Norris out to Australia for a tour, and after [Bob and Chuck] became immediate friends, [Chuck] said to me that if I ever made it to California, I should look him up and we could do some training together. So when I arrived on these shores, of course the first person I called was Chuck. That led to a starring role in the movie The Octagon as the main baddie Kyo, the masked enforcer.

I ended up doing both security work and movies for quite a number of years, but when I finally started thinking about the safety and mortality aspects of the bodyguard work I was doing, I thought to myself that it was probably a good time to stop. I had had two friends who got shot and killed doing similar security work, and while I'd managed to avoid being shot or stabbed or anything grue-

Photo courtesy Adrian Carr

some like that, I always knew that there are no guarantees, and that it was always a remote possibility. So around the mid-90s I decided it was time to stop the work on the road, and just focus on the movies.

Now [my bodyguard career] just feels like another lifetime to me. I always laughingly say to friends that traveling around the world with some of the biggest rock 'n roll bands of the 70s and 80s, being treated almost like a member of the group, well, it just doesn't get any better than that! So much fun, madness and extravagance. It really was such an amazing time in my life, with memories that I will forever cherish.

The Key to Success

Before I finish, one thing I want to stress that I learnt is that the one thing that people at the top of their game — and this doesn't just apply to the rock acts I toured with, but also to people like Chuck

Norris and Jackie Chan — the one thing they have in common is an incredible passion for what they do.

You need to understand that you don't get to be someone like a Jagger, a Taylor, a Ronstadt or a Chuck Norris without forever-ever searching for ways to better yourself. There was never a time that Jagger wasn't thinking of ways to increase his stage presence, or Lindsey Buckingham wasn't strumming his guitar trying to find a different note or a different song, or Linda Ronstadt wasn't trying to find a new voice coach to help her hit a different note. The incredible artists like the ones I had the privilege of working for who sustained such longevity in their careers, they're the ones who were always endlessly striving to better themselves, to raise the bar.

Those people taught me to never accept mediocrity in anything I did. For that lesson, I am forever grateful.

@rjbromleynorton

@rjnorton64

www.richardnorton.org

Chapter Fifteen

HASSAN "MVP" ASSAD

Photo courtesy Hassan Assad.

"Jex told us,'Tonight, zere is no diplomacy! Zey are animals, so we will treat zem like animals!'"

If ever there were a poster boy for turning your life around, it would be former World Wrestling Entertainment (WWE) super-star Hassan Assad aka "MVP".

Florida native Assad's beginnings were not promising, as he was drawn into gang life at the young age of fourteen. At sixteen, he was brought up on charges of armed robbery and kidnapping following a shotgun-slinging, *Ocean's 11*-style cruise ship heist that netted him an 18 1/2 year prison sentence.

While incarcerated he met a corrections officer who dabbled as an independent wrestler, and after good behavior saw Assad gain his release in just under a decade, he took the officer up on an offer to help him get into the business.

After five years on the American indies and a short stint in Puerto Rico, Assad signed a WWE developmental deal in 2005. It took him less than a year to earn a call-up to the main roster, where he debuted as arrogant blue-chip athlete Montel Vontavious Porter.

A successful run followed, until Assad requested his release with a year still left on his contract in order to fulfill his dream of wrestling in Japan. Shortly afterward he signed with New Japan Pro Wrestling, which became his home for the next two years.

Assad's eventual return to the USA saw him join TNA/IMPACT Wrestling for a short run as one of the company's top stars before returning to the indies.

Assad has also released a number of hip-hop videos, competes in Brazilian jiu-jitsu tournaments, and has plans to open a wrestling-themed bar in Houston, Texas.

Street-Certified

I got out of prison in July, 1999. Coming home after spending almost a decade in prison I found that most people don't want to hire convicted felons, so it was difficult for me to find work. A few people suggested to me, "You're a pretty big guy, you know how to handle yourself, have you ever considered bouncing?" It had never crossed my mind, but now [finding work] was a matter of survival, so I said, "Yeah, I'll take whatever I can get."

I started off making $65 a night at a little Jamaican reggae party, and then I made my way down to South Beach [Florida]. I went down to a club on Washington Avenue called The Living Room, one of the most exclusive, high-end clubs at the time. There was this big, bearded guy standing outside and I introduced myself, asked him if they were hiring. He told me his name was Kevin, then introduced me to a guy named Eric who was running security. I ended up getting hired and working there on a regular basis with the bearded guy, who went on to be known as [street fighting legend/MMA superstar] Kimbo Slice.

At that particular club we only had to break up a few fights, because it was usually high-end, wealthy people. But on occasion we had to deal with someone. One night, we had just closed the club — it used to close at 5 AM, so this would have been five-fifteenish — and we were collecting all the bouncers' radios and having a little post-work meeting. You know, chillin' , havin' a beer. Then there was a knock on the door, and I opened it up and saw this cop named John who we all knew real well. I'm not exactly sure if the club gave him a little kickback to hang around outside, but he was around a lot and the club had a relationship with him.

I see that John is with two South American Hispanic guys. I've never seen these guys before in my life, but one of 'em points at me and says, "That's him! That's the guy who hit me!" John looks at me and says, "Is that true, did you hit this guy?" and I say, "That's bullshit! I've never seen this guy before, I have no idea what he's talking about." I'm standing just inside the doorway with the cop and the two Hispanic guys just outside, and as we're talking I look to my left. From behind one of the plants that's set up inside the club, I see Kimbo poke his head out, put his finger to his lips, and go *"Shhhhhhh!"* (laughs)

MVP and the late, great Kimbo Slice (Photo courtesy Hassan Assad)

You gotta be *kiddin'* me! So Kimbo punched this guy in the face, and now I'm talking to John and thinking, "How hard did Kimbo hit this dude that he thinks it was ME?" How do you make that mistake? I mean, I know there are some that say [black people] all look alike, but you can't tell me that if you saw me and Kimbo standing together in a lineup, you couldn't identify him from me! (laughs) I think you should be able to make that distinction.

Fortunately, we had a decent working relationship with John so I didn't get into any trouble. I just told him, "Look at my hands, I didn't punch anybody," and added that I could get a bunch of people to say I hadn't even been outside all night. So the cop ended up just telling that guy to fuck off, and it all blew over.

Stephon Marbury

After a while, I moved up Washington Avenue to take a position as assistant head of security at a club called Mansion. With this being South Beach, we had tons of celebrities coming through and for the most part, most of 'em were cool. But once in a while you'd get some dipshit, and one of those dipshits was [NBA All-star] Stephon Marbury.

One night, Marbury's standing outside the rope with a girl and his bodyguard. This is a dressy club, but he's got on a t-shirt, denim shorts and sneakers. Not even fresh sneakers, too — they weren't even right out the box! But because this is Stephon Marbury, he feels that we're supposed to let him into the club. He's tellin' the front-door man — a little, short French guy who I was pretty cool with — Marbury's tellin' him, "Hey, don't make this mistake, man. Don't make this mistake." The French guy just says, "I am sorry, I cannot let you in ze club, you do not have ze proper dress code."

Marbury keeps sayin', "You about to make a big mistake, man. Don't make this mistake." Now, I don't know if he's a nice guy or not, but that night he was just being a douche and it was totally unnecessary. Finally I couldn't help myself, and I stepped up and said, "Make WHAT mistake? You tell me, WHAT mistake? Really? YOU, dude? YOU threatening somebody?" I don't fancy myself a tough guy but I can look after myself, and I'm just like, "Nah, dude, this ain't goin' down. I DARE you to step across that rope!"

At that moment, management intervened and conversations were had, and they asked me to go back into the club so I don't know what was resolved. But as I walked back in I couldn't stop thinking, "Stephon *MARBURY*? Really?!" (laughs)

Subsequently, I was on Opie and Anthony when [WWE] had the Royal Rumble at Madison Square Garden, and I told that story. They

MVP with mixed martial arts legend Kazushi Sakuraba (Photo courtesy Hassan Assad)

thought it was pretty funny, and then one of 'em said, "Wait a second, aren't you guys performing in the Garden this weekend?" Because that's the home of the Knicks, who Marbury was playing for at the time. Now, I'm a big Knicks fan, but I laughed and said, "Yes, I will be at Madison Square Garden this weekend, and if [Marbury] has a problem with my story, he can come and see me in the dressing room."

I never heard a peep about it. But who knows? Maybe he did show up but didn't have the right dress code! (laughs)

Iron Mike

On another night at Mansion, I saw none other than the legendary Mike Tyson walking into the men's restroom. He had a guy with him who was acting as his security, and also a guy who I knew was a cocaine dealer. Now, it's South Beach, people are there to party. I'm not the police, [so my attitude was] have a good time, just keep your shit low-key.

I go into the bathroom, and this guy who I knew to be a coke dealer and Mike Tyson are in a stall together. I look at Mike's security and say, "Hey, do me a favor. Go on down there and tell them that the two of 'em can't be in that stall together." But the guy just looks at me and says, "YOU tell 'em." Well, now. (laughs)

Okay, I'm thinking this through. I'm gonna go down here and tell MIKE TYSON that he can't be in the stall like that? I mean, if he's upset, and he comes out of that stall and punches me in my shit... but then I thought that if I take a shot from Mike Tyson, then really it's a W because as far as the bouncers in South Beach are concerned, I'm the man! Like maybe there's some weird kind of honor to be found in that:

"Hassan fought *MIKE TYSON?*"

"Yeah! He got his jaw broken, but he fought 'im! That's wassup!" (laughs)

On the flipside, I'm thinking that if he does get belligerent, I could probably double-leg [takedown] his ass. He's got nasty hands, but I don't know what his ground game is like. We're at close quarters in the bathroom, so I might be able double-leg him, take him down until I get some help. All of this is running through my head, until finally I take a deep breath and I'm like, "All right, here we go."

I knock on the bathroom stall, the door opens up, and I catch them in mid-transaction. The guy who's a coke dealer, he sees me right away and his eyes are like, "Oh, shit!" Then I see Mike, and I'm like, "Hey, man. The two of you can't be in the stall like that."

And I wait for the fallout.

But Mike just looks at me and says, "Aw man, I'm so sorry! I apologize, I didn't mean to violate your rules or anything. No problem, man, we'll step out. I apologize." I was so disarmed by that result when I was expecting something more belligerent, I found myself going, "You know, there's a special owner's box called Level Six up at the top of the club, where just the ultra-ultra VIPs get to party. I'll get you up there so you can have a little privacy." And Mike was just awesome about it, "Thank you so much, man. I appreciate that, thank you!" I got one of my guys and said, "Hey, man, you stay with Mike. Take him on up to Level Six and get him whatever he needs. Make sure he's taken care of, and keep me posted."

Maybe an hour or so later, I stop by Level Six to see how Mike's doin'. When I walk in, blunts are burnin', people are partyin', there's chicks up there, it's business as usual. Mike sees me and comes over, and I say, "You all right? Everything's cool?" He just gives me a big hug, then reaches in his pocket and peels off a few hundred-dollar bills, puts 'em in my hand and says, "Man, thank you so much for treating me like a human being. I appreciate that, thank you." That's a direct quote, I remember every word.

Mike was just awesome. [The situation was] totally the opposite of what I was expecting to happen — which would have been tragic for me — and it turned out to be a really cool experience. This was not too long after Mike had been released from prison and people were really down on him, but even at that point of his life, he was still a really good dude.

Years later, I had the opportunity to talk to Mike and his son backstage at Monday Night Raw, and I reminded him that we'd met on South Beach. He asked me to tell him what happened, and I said, "Well, I don't know if that's something I want to discuss in front of your son." But he said, "No, no — tell me in front of my son! He needs to learn, he needs to know about this kind of stuff." And that's why I feel okay telling this story, because he was so open about the way he used to be, even with his son there.

I'm glad he's doing much better now, getting through his trials and tribulations. Iron Mike is truly one of my heroes for being able to make it through [tough times], bounce back, and conduct himself as a gentleman.

Khaled's Birthday Massacre

Every year, DJ Khaled would have his birthday party at Mansion. A funny little tie-in is that when I first started bouncing at that little reggae spot, [Khaled] was the lowest-on-the-totem-pole opening DJ there. Fast forward, and here we are a few years later and he's one of the moguls of the Miami hip-hop scene. Me, Khaled, and Kimbo Slice — we all came out of the same scene at the same time, starting out with nothing and becoming fortunate enough to make it in our respective fields.

Anyway, every year Khaled's birthday party was a Who's Who of hip-hop, rappers and their entourages. More often than not, the rappers would be pretty cool, but their entourages could be out of control sometimes. And that meant that it wasn't a matter of "if" something was gonna happen, it was a matter of "when" and "how bad".

One year in the early 2000s, a fight broke out at Khaled's party that quickly became a full-blown riot. At South Beach, the police never go into the clubs — NEVER — but this got so bad that police had to go in because it was beyond the security's ability to control. And after they did, a police officer got hit in the head with a magnum of champagne. I think he nearly died, and the injury forced him into retirement.

After that, [Mansion] started bringing in a French Canadian guy named Jex, a fighter who was one of the owner's personal security. And for that one night, Jex would import a bunch of guys with him from a fight academy in downtown Miami called Fight Club.

Normally at Mansion we wore suits and ties, but on DJ Khaled's birthday it was jeans and t-shirts. Like I said, it wasn't a matter of "if", but "when" and "how bad", so just like in a Bunkhouse [pro wrestling] match, we came dressed appropriately! (laughs)

I remember during one pre-night meeting, Jex telling us in his French accent, "Tonight, zere is no diplomacy! Zey are animals, so we will treat zem like animals!" Meaning zero tolerance, stomp that shit out. As soon as some-body gets out of line, react violently and stuff it. Now, that goes against everything that any effective, reputable, respectable bouncer would do — you always try to be an effective communicator [and employ] conflict reso-lution without violence. But unfortunately, the crowd that was comin' in that night, they're not tryin' to talk, they're not tryin' to hear you. The only thing they really responded to, unfortunately, was violence.

It don't mean a thing if you ain't got dat BLING. (Photo courtesy WrightWayPhotography.com)

Later on, it was just packed with every rapper and entourage, including an out-of-town rap group that had ties to a big drug gang. We'd had issues with that gang, they would come into South Beach and literally take over clubs. Come in thirty, forty deep, reserve a bunch of tables, buy tons of bottles of champagne and just take the place over.

At one point, those guys insisted that they wanted to get their art-ist up on the stage. Unfortunately, the passage that leads to the stage was already packed, and onstage there was way too many people as it was. Everybody wanted to get onstage so they could be seen — that was the place, that was the prime real estate for the night. And that's also where I was standing with my buddy Attila, who was on the Swedish Olympic boxing team and also fought pro for a while. Attila was probably six-seven, maybe two-sixty-five or two-seventy. Great guy, had an overhand right like a howitzer.

Attila and I were standing there, and the main guy in [the gang's] crew, this little guy — it's always the little guy who's doing all the fucking barking — he was like, "We're comin' on back there, we're comin' onstage." I was like, "Nope, you guys aren't comin' back here." But he kept it up, "Move, we comin' through!" I told him again, "There's no room back here, you gotta turn around." But still he begged to differ... and that was very unfortunate. (laughs)

Attila had on leather gloves with the pulverized dust in the knuckles, you know? And I had a set of brass knuckles in each pocket. So I got on the radio and called it in, let the other security know that we had an incident. Said, "Everybody respond," because I knew from my experience that this was gonna be that incident that set it off.

It was about to go down.

Attila looked at me and said, "Say when." I reached in my pocket, put my brass knuckles on and told 'em one last time, "You ain't going onstage." Then the first punch was thrown, and there it was. CHAOS. Hennessy bottles flying, one guy had a stanchion that he was swinging, and Attila was literally — and I'm not exaggerating at all — droppin' dudes one punch at a time. Right, left, right, left, cuttin' a path through the crowd. I'm right there with him, and at one point I look up and see this French [bouncer] named Patrick, a Muay Thai kickboxer, come flying through the air and his knee SMASHES this dude right in the face! It was beautiful, like something out of a movie. Van Damme would have been proud! (laughs)

At Khaled's party, the lights never come on and the music never stops. But at this point the lights *did* come on and the music *did* stop because of past incidents and how bad they had gotten. I don't remember exactly how it happened, but we were eventually able to, to borrow a phrase, effectively crush the insurrection. When it was over, there were literally bodies strewn outside in various states of consciousness.

Then I saw that one guy who started it, the one who refused to accept, "No, we don't have room, you can't go onstage." [He was] lying in the back parking lot and he still had his Timberland boots on, had his boxers on, had his shirt on... but his pants were gone and he was rollin' on the ground, crying! I don't know how it happened, but somehow one of our guys literally beat the pants off that dude! (laughs)

Fortunately our side took no losses, nobody was injured. Maybe a black eye or a split lip, but nobody required any medical care. [Afterwards] there was this collective sigh of relief, because when you're dealing with that element, you don't know if guns are gonna come out, or if people are gonna be comin' in the back door... you just don't know how bad it's gonna be. But fortunately, that night it got real bad real fast, then it was crushed, everything was done, and it was back to the party.

Party On

One time I caught this chick in the VIP section, getting fucked. Not hiding either, there was no hiding goin' on! I walked by and saw a dude just fuckin' nailin' her, right there on the couch. People are dancin', music's playin', there's a group with them, they got bottles, and I'm like, "Really? Just like that?" Under normal circumstances I'd be like, "Hey, man — you guys got to take that shit outside." But it was so brazen that I was taken aback. And I just kept right on movin', thinking, "You know what? Party on." (laughs) I wasn't even gonna stop that — it would be a great story for them to tell one day.

MVP captures gold at the Houston International BJJ Open (Photo courtesy Hassan Assad)

Shannen Doherty

There was a guy who came to work with us, I don't remember his name, but he was good. A good-lookin' guy, and whenever there was an issue, he was always standin' there tall. Never in the back, always side-by-side [with the rest of us].

So Shannen Doherty came to the club one night, and I told him, "You stay with Shannen, keep an eye on her and if you need anything, you let me know." Later on, I swing by the VIP to check on things, and I see brother and Shannen Doherty makin' out! Now, at the time I'm the assistant head of security, so I'm supposed to tell the guy, "You can't do that." He's supposed to be in trouble. But, you know... the man in me just couldn't hate! (laughs) I couldn't bring myself to go over there and say, "Hey, what are you doing?"

So after a few minutes, I passed back through and I slid up to him and said, "Hey, bro — keep it together." And he said "Cool," so I went to the front door and posted up there, keeping an eye on things. After a few minutes, brother calls me on the radio and says that Shannen Doherty is on her way out, they're moving to the front. But when they get there, he's got his shirt unbuttoned, his tie is off, and he's leavin' too!

Maybe another boss would have said, "You can't leave! You're fired!" But all I could say was, "Hey, you know what? See you next week, brother. I hope you seal the deal." (laughs)

@The305MVP

@truly_mvp

Chapter Sixteen

ANDY McPHEE

All photos courtesy Andy McPhee.

"I must have hit him in the perfect spot because he just stood there like a mannequin, totally unconscious."

Over his quarter-century-plus career in show business, Australia's Andy McPhee has graced the big and small screens in well over 100 productions including the feature film *Saving Mr. Banks,* the chilling *Wolf Creek* miniseries, and the long-running soap operas *Neighbours* and *Home and Away.*

His most famous role to date came in the TV series *Sons of Anarchy* as Keith McGee, president of the eponymous motorcycle club's Belfast chapter.

Still going strong in his career's third decade, Andy both works and teaches in his adopted hometown of Los Angeles.

Bad Penny

I used to bounce in a club in Adelaide [Australia]. It was a pretty dark sort of club, had a big, thick glass security door at the front. You got some pretty colorful characters in there — a lot of bikers used to hang out, local gangsters, strippers and stuff. A pretty mixed bag, you know?

One night I was standing out front, leaning against a parking meter. It was pretty cold out, but since I didn't smoke I'd often stay outside because I couldn't stand the smoke [in the bar]. These three lads come down the street, and they didn't catch on that I was the bouncer so they just walked past me and tried to open the front door. They're pushing on the door, trying to get it open, and then one of them steps back and gives it a really good kick. So I go up and say, "What are you doing, mate?" and he asks who I am. I tell him I'm security, but he just tells me to fuck off, right?

So I went to grab him and he ran. Now I'm chasing him — I'm being a goose, don't even know why I wasted my time — and he slipped and fell down and I fell on top of him. Bad luck for me, because there was cops across the other side of the road watching the whole thing, except all they saw was me chasing a guy and landing on him!

So I jumped up, went back inside, told me boss what happened and said, "Look, I'm gonna take off for a bit 'cause [the guy is] already talking to the cops." I had long hair at the time [that I wore] pulled back into a ponytail, so I let my hair down, put my

Andy during his pro wrestling days as "Mad Max Miller"

spare set of clothes on and went for a walk out in the street, stayed away for a while.

Nothing happened right away, but a few days later I get a notice in the mail that I've gotta go to court. I'm up for Common Assault, which is the lowest assault [charge] you'll ever get, it's just like pushing someone. That cost me a few hundred bucks. Jeez.

A couple weeks later I'm at the front again, just inside the door, and I happen to be talking to a friend of mine who was a cowboy from up in Darwin. His job was to rope cows and bulls, a pretty hardcore sort of bloke, right? So at one point I look down the street, and who do I see but the guy who I got the assault charge for chasing! I go to my friend, "Aw, shit. Here comes that guy again, and he's got his two mates with 'im. Listen, I can't touch him now, can you go out and tell 'im to piss off? Hopefully he won't be a smart-ass like last time and give you a mouthful."

So my mate told him he can't come in, and sure enough, the guy give 'im a mouthful. So my mate give 'im a bit of a slap 'round the chops, right? Then I opened the front door and told the bloke,

"You just never know who you're gonna run into, do ya?" (laughs) And off the guy goes down the street again.

This next part is 100% true, swear to God.

A couple of hours later, me and my mate are still out front and I'm standing with my back to the street. Next thing I know, this little beer bottle — we call 'em stubbies — goes flying past my head and hits the wall beside me! It lands on the ground without breaking, so without having any idea who threw it or why, I snatch it up, spin around, and throw it right back in the direction it come from. Well, it turns out that bottle was chucked out of a car that was cruising past with that dickhead hanging out the passenger side, and my completely unaimed throw hit 'im straight in the head! (laughs) I would never, never have been able to do it if I tried, mate! But I clocked him straight in the head, and the car carried on down the street and it was all done, right? Finished.

But not quite.

Now it's two weeks later. I'm finishing work and I go to catch a cab home... and you'll never fuckin' guess who's drivin' the cab, mate! (laughs) I just thought, "I'm gonna say nothin' about it, but I'm not gonna let him drop me at home so he knows where I live." I'm just talking away, leading him down the garden path and having a happy old conversation while pretending that I don't know who he is. I'm a bitch, because I stretched it out as long as I could! (laughs)

Finally I say, "That's my house, here" — it wasn't — and I paid him the money and got out. But as soon as I shut my door, I quickly grabbed the handle of the driver's door, pulled it open, leaned right into the guy's face and yelled, *"YOU LITTLE COCK-*

SUCKER! I KNOW WHO YOU ARE, SO STOP RUNNING INTO ME AND FUCK OFF!"

That shook him up pretty good, and after I shut the door he just sat there for about two minutes, not doing anything. I honestly think he pissed himself! (laughs)

Act Like an Asshole, Get Slapped Like an Asshole

I did a bit a judo, I was a black belt, and I did pro wrestling for twenty years. But I can tell you, mate — you put me in the ring with someone and I'll shit meself. I was a grappler and all that sort of stuff, but I wasn't really good at boxing. I did it, but I hated getting hit in the head, couldn't stand it. I was not what I would say is a really tough guy, or a ballsy stand-up [fighter], but I did all right when I had to.

I had this little technique I learned off my judo mates, a bit of a jaw-slap. You cup your hand and you hit 'em between the ear and the bottom of the jaw. You don't even have to hit 'em hard to knock 'em out. I couldn't believe it, you just clip 'em on the side of the face and they would slowly sink to the ground. So you didn't have to really hurt anyone if you got into a situation.

One night, I was standing out the front [of the club] and I had my girl with me. She's now my ex, the mother of my kids, but at the time we'd just met. She and her friend were beside me, just talking to me, and there's about three or four blokes standing in front of me too, just talkin'. Then these other big guys come walkin' down the street, and one of 'em started asking me about the club. I could tell that they were country boys from up the bush, and knowing that those guys can be pretty loud and cause a ruckus, I said, "Ah, it's probably not your deal, mate. You'll end up gettin' into trouble in there." So the guy says, "Okay, fair enough. But what about the sluts?" I say, "What sluts?" and he says, "The ones standing there beside you."

Well, fuck. (laughs)

I just reached over the guys I'd been talking to, and give the bloke this little slap in the face. It wasn't very hard at all but it must have touched the perfect spot, because after it connected the guy just stood there like a mannequin, completely unconscious! Then he finally folded like an elevator, sat down really slowly and sank to the ground with the cigarette still in his hand. A few seconds later he woke up, looked up at me and calmly said, "Fuck, that was cool!" (laughs)

The Final Straw

On another night I'm standin' out front as I normally do, and these two big guys come out. They're the same height as me, six-foot-six, and they have really short hair so I figure they're either military guys or cops. They're walking out with their beers and I try to say, "Sorry guys, you'll have to go back in and drink 'em," but they push past me before I can even finish. So I say again, "Guys, you can't come out here with a beer because the club will lose its license. There's cops patrolling the street here."

One of the guys just looked at me, stepped back, took this little stance and raised the bottle to head height. I thought, "No, you're not going to throw that at me, surely," but I took a step back in case he did. And he did, he he threw it! Thankfully I got out of the way, and then I grabbed him and shoved him to the ground.

Then I made a mistake, I didn't bother to restrain the other guy. I thought, "Aw, he's too drunk, he'll be alright." But he was sober enough to grab me by the right arm, and then the other dude's up and he grabs me by the other arm! So here I am, hanging on tight to both of them, thinking, "Fuck, I can't let 'em go or they'll start whacking into me." I finally manage to push the guy who I shoved before, and he goes down again before the other guy drives me hard up against a window. I heard the window split, and thought, "Fuck, this is not good. I've gotta get out of here." All I could think about was jagged bits of glass dropping into me neck. So I pushed off the window, ran the guy into a parked car, and his head knocked against it and stunned him a little bit. But then his mate came up and grabbed me again.

So here I am up against the car, my arms locked together with these guys like we're dancin', and then I notice [a group of bystanders] lookin' at me and I go, "Can one of yous go inside and get the other bouncer, PLEASE?!" (laughs) Right after that, I let one of the guys go and pushed him back down to the concrete, then put my hand over the other one's face and shoved him backward over the bonnet of the car before letting go and backing up. I wasn't throwing punches or elbows yet, because I'm not one of those guys who just want to beat people to death. These blokes were so drunk that I didn't really see any reason to hit them, and sure enough, after they got up they both decided that they were not up for causing any more trouble.

Then I looked back at the window I'd been shoved into, and just like I thought, there were big slivers of glass just hanging down. I watched as a couple of 'em fell to the ground and shattered, and realized that they would have slit my neck right open, you know?

I went inside to tell the other bouncer to come out in case there was any more bother, but when I came back out again, the two guys were both laid out on the sidewalk, completely unconscious! I thought, "What the fuck happened here?" and then I turned around and saw a friend of mine, a crazy, skinny little guy who I knew from [working at] the railways, and I said, "What did you do?" He said, "Well, after you went inside

they were being a bit smart, so I had to have a word with both of 'em."
(laughs) Fuck, mate! I shook 'em both a little bit until they woke up, and
then looked at the bigger of the two guys and said, "Dude, seriously — all
you had to do was go back inside and drink your beer. But look at you
now!" He was so drunk and stunned from the slap my mate had given
him that he couldn't even respond.

That was pretty much it for me, I give up [bouncing] shortly after
that. I was about forty at the time, and still bouncin' at forty, that's way
too old. It's too dangerous. It doesn't matter how good you are, there's
always that one punk who's going to pull something out and use it. And
when they start doing shit like that, it's just not worth it.

@ *www.imdb.com/name/nm0574173/?ref_=ttfc_fc_cl_t16*

Chapter Seventeen

JASON "DOOMS" DAY

Photo courtesy DavidFordPictures.com

"You can't choke a girl out... no matter how much you might want to."

A true trailblazer of Canadian mixed martial arts, Jason "Dooms" Day has nearly a decade of in-the-cage action under his belt against such names as David "The Crow" Loiseau, Jonathan "The Road Warrior" Goulet, and UFC middleweight champion Michael "The Count" Bisping.

After a rocky 3-5 start to his MMA career, Day went on a rampage winning fourteen of his next sixteen fights. This earned him a shot in the Ultimate Fighting Championship, where he shocked the world with a TKO victory over the heavily-favored Alan Belcher at the first UFC event ever held on Canadian soil.

In 2012, injuries from a traffic accident forced Day to set the four-ounce gloves aside and focus on a new career as an actor/stuntman. His rapidly-expanding resume includes roles in the feature film *Deadpool,* the hit TV series *Arrow,* and the much-lauded *EA Sports UFC* video game.

Torture Chambers and The Grampinator

I first started bouncing in Lethbridge, Alberta. [Fighter/trainer/ promoter] Lee "The Grampinator" Mein got me my first few jobs, and he's also the guy who got me into jiu-jitsu and MMA. I'm a big guy and a little bit intimidating, but I'm also mild-mannered, so Lee figured I'd be good as a doorman and also a good guy to learn jiu-jitsu. Meeting Lee was the point where my fight career really took off.

Lee was a great doorman because he's from the OLD old-school. He knows how to really fight, and he's huge, and he doesn't put up with any shit. When the gangs started moving down from Calgary, we were all worried, "Oooh, they carry knives and shit." But Lee wouldn't even hesitate, he'd just walk outside and start smashing guys! (laughs) I'm actually glad he's out of [bouncing] now, because time was not on his side. When you're that fearless, sooner or later one of these guys is gonna pull a knife or gun on you and it's game over.

So anyway, one night these girls started fighting. Slapping each other and screaming, you know how it goes. When I went in there and broke it up, one of the girls started being a total bitch, yipping at both me and the other chick. Then the boyfriends came over, but the boyfriend of the one who was trippin' just stood back and let her go. She kept chirping and chirping at me, even after the other chick's boyfriend had taken her away.

My good buddy [and fellow MMA fighter] Dan "Torture" Chambers was also working that night, and he came over and said, "Jay, what's the problem?" I said, "This chick won't shut up, man," so Dan looked at the boyfriend and asked, "Is this your girl?" The guy had barely responded "Yes" when — *BANG!* — Dan open-hand cuffed him right in the head and said, *"CONTROL YOUR BITCH!"* (laughs) The boyfriend was shell-shocked and didn't do a thing, but the girl LOST IT. I had to drag her out of there because she was going insane, while her boyfriend just walked out behind us, all embarrassed.

But that's back in the day — I don't wanna think about how long ago it was — when you could get away with stuff like that. Lethbridge is oil country, lots of rednecks and a large Native Canadian population [that are] always clashing with each other. It wasn't until the end of my bouncing days that all the legal stuff started coming into play, but before that, you never saw people screaming about pressing charges. It was a rough kind of town where anything went, and we did whatever we had to do.

Torture to the Rescue

Dan got me out of a lot of sticky situations, far more than I ever got him out of. One night I was outside in the parking lot, dealing with these guys who were a little older than me, and HUGE. Looked like they'd been juicin' [taking steroids] for a few years. I was still only twenty-two or so, and this was before I had much experience in any

Jason makes his way to the Hardcore Championship Fighting cage.
(Photo courtesy AndrasSchram.com)

kind of martial arts or contact sports, so dealing with these guys was a real problem. And it was made worse by the fact that I was the only doorman outside at the time.

Somehow I got wedged between two cars, with one of the guys on each side. This wasn't like they were trying to fight each other and I was breaking it up, they were both trying to get ME. So I ducked and covered, thinking, "This is the end," when I suddenly heard this banging noise getting louder — *toonk-toonk-TOONK-TOONK!* That turned out to be the sound of Dan running along the top of one of the cars and leaving footprints in the metal!

Like something out of the movies, he came flying off [the car] with a Superman punch and *BANG,* knocked one of the guys out cold! Then he turned around and KOed the other guy with a big haymaker. One moment it looked like I was finished, the next moment there was these two huge guys just laid out, and I'm thinking, "Okay, Dan... you're my new best friend!" (laughs)

New-Age Bouncing

One night before our shift started, the bar brought in a lawyer to let us know the legal way to deal with customers. "Excuse me sir, we're gonna have to ask you to leave the property. If you don't, we shall have to use force to move you off the premises." That kind of stuff.

At the end of the night we had this guy who didn't want to leave. An oil worker with tons of cash, wearing fancy clothes and flashing a nice gold Rolex but redneck as fuck. I guess you would call him a Rig Pig — or maybe I shouldn't say that — um, let's say "roughneck". Not an executive or anything, but he had some money like all those guys do. Basically, a barbarian all cleaned up.

So me and Dan decided that we were gonna implement the fancy-pants lawyer's strategy, and we said, "Sir, if you don't move, we're going to have to gently escort you out." Of course he wasn't having it, so we each took an arm and escorted him out, not rough or anything. He was fighting the whole way, yelling, *"LET GO OF ME! LET GO OF ME!"*, but there was two of us and one of him, so it wasn't really a big problem

When we got him to the bottom of the stairs his Rolex came unclasped and kind of fell off, and the guy just LOST IT as if somebody shot his dog or something. He started swinging at us but me and Dan just stayed straight-faced, catching his hands and holding them. "Sir, if you don't calm down, we will have to apply a little more force."

I finally tripped him and lowered him gently to the ground, then I took his ID out of his pocket to record who he was, all the stuff that the lawyer told us to do. But after we finally let the guy go, he still called the cops on us and we had to explain the whole thing to the officers. That was the first time that we'd done things so strictly, and I'll tell you, it was HORRIBLE. I hated having to do things that way.

My Go-To

My favorite technique was to just walk up, grab a [problem customer] and choke him out. Wait till he went limp, set him down, drag him outside. Some guys would wake up really calm, other guys would wake up freakin' out, but either way I found that was the best way to handle shit. Choke 'em out and get 'em out — nobody breaks anything, you don't get a black eye or cracked ribs, no lawsuits, nothing. The only bad thing was that when you choked a guy out in front of girls, they'd always start screaming, "YOU KILLED HIM!!!", and then THEY'D start swinging, hitting you with their purse or whatever. And you can't choke a girl out... no matter how much you might want to. (laughs)

Stampede Stupidity

In 2011, I was head doorman for the Wild Horse tent at the Calgary Stampede. [The Stampede is] one of the biggest parties in Calgary, and the Wild Horse tent has a capacity of a thousand people. During Stampede Week, things are CRAZY — people drink for a week straight starting at ten every morning, so all sorts of shit happens.

I would always stay at the front entrance and control the lineup, which was a full-time job because we had two, three, sometimes four-hour lineups with hundreds of people waiting to get in. I would

Jason leaves the cage with his big, fat belly hanging out everywhere. Gross.
(Photo courtesy AndrasSchram.com)

stand with my back against a fence that surrounded the tent, and on the other side of the fence there was a patio where people who'd gotten in could go out and drink. There was a big Corona banner across the [top half of the] fence, which made it so you could only see the people on the patio from the waist down.

One day I was at my usual post, talking with the other bouncers, and all of a sudden they started backing away from me and laughing. I didn't know what was going on until I looked over my shoulder and saw a jetstream of who-knew-what kind of liquid shooting past me from behind the banner! So I peeked underneath it and saw that this girl had pulled her up dress, pulled down her panties, grabbed her ankles, and launched this firehose stream of piss through the fence! There was piss EVERYWHERE — all over a table, all over the banner, I mean, this chick had to *go!* And when she was done, she just casually hiked her underwear up, pulled her dress down, picked her beer back up and started drinking again, standing in a pool of her own piss! That's the kind of thing that happens all the time at Stampede, people just drink beyond stupidity.

Entourage

Another time at about eleven-thirty on a Friday night, the party's pumpin' and the place is packed and we can't fit any more people. People had been lined up for hours, three or four hundred of 'em. Suddenly, this lady walks to the front of the line all in a huff, and she says, "You better get us in right away!" I say, "I'm sorry, lady, but I don't know who you are." She says, "I have Adrian Grenier and a whole entourage with me, and we're supposed to have VIP service!" Not recognizing the name and not knowing any better, I say, "I'm sorry, I don't have this Adrian person on my list — who is she?" (laughs) The lady says, "It's a *he!* He's the star of *Entourage!*"

Now, I never really watched that show so I still didn't know who this Adrian guy was, but I wanted to help. So I said, "I don't have you on my list, but let me call my boss and see what I can do." But even though I'm trying to help her, she keeps on being a bit of a bitch, really high maintenance. So even though I eventually click in to who Adrian Grenier is, since this chick has pissed me off I keep referring to him as "she":

"I'm sorry, lady, but you're going to have to take her and her crew around back."

"It's a *GUY!* Adrian Grenier, the TV star!"

"I'm sorry, ma'am, I've just never heard of her." (laughs)

Jason accidentally punts his good friend David "The Crow" Loiseau right inna goober during their 2008 clash. (Photo courtesy AndrasSchram.com)

This chick is getting SO upset, and she finally says, "If you don't get us in RIGHT NOW, we're gonna take HIM down to Cowboy's," which is the other big place in town.

I just say, "Look, lady, we're packed to the rafters. And even if I let you in, there's no benefit to the bar because we're probably going to have to promo your tab, seeing as you're all famous and everything."

But finally my boss came up and started apologizing to her like crazy. I just turned to him and said, "Why suck up to this lady?" But hey, if that's what he wanted to do, then whatever. I just found the whole thing to be ridiculous.

🐦 *@jasonwilliamday*
📷 *@jasonwilliamday*

Chapter Eighteen

AARON RILEY

Photo courtesy Aaron Riley.

"The driver started swerving all over the road with the drunk guy clinging onto the hood and yelling."

Any serious discussion about mixed martial arts history must include the Indiana-based HOOKnSHOOT organization, which spearheaded the worldwide women's MMA scene and gave a start to future UFC champions Dave Menne, Frank Mir, and Miesha "Cupcake" Tate. And when talking about HOOKnSHOOT, one cannot help but mention that group's figurehead fighter, the iron-jawed Aaron Riley.

After making his professional combat debut while still in high school, Riley went on to compete in nearly every prominent MMA organization in the world including PRIDE, Shooto, IFL, bodog-FIGHT, and the UFC.

A product of the wild 1990s, Riley once fought nine times in the space of a year before making his Octagon debut at UFC 37 against future welterweight champion "Ruthless" Robbie Lawler. To this day, that bout stands as one of the greatest battles that the sport of MMA has ever seen.

If you're a newer fan and Riley's name doesn't sound familiar to you, it's worth taking a few minutes to look him up. While he will probably never get the level of credit that he deserves, it's an inarguable fact that Riley's blood-and-guts style played a major role in increasing the popularity of MMA during its formative years.

The Irish Immigrant

In an unusual way, security work started early for me. I started to fight [professionally] super young — I started kickboxing when I was 14 and MMA when I was 16, plus I was on my high school wrestling team. So all the time, people I went to high school with would want me to back them up like I was their ace in the hole. They'd routinely ring my doorbell while they were on their way to fight somebody, asking me to come along and back them up.

Later on, after I moved to Kirkland, Washington and began training at AMC Kickboxing, a buddy of mine who was moving out of town gave me his [bouncing] job at a place in Seattle called The Irish Immigrant. The place was aptly named because when I started, I think I was the only American working there — almost everyone else was an actual transplant from Ireland. Those guys were always ready to throw down at the drop of a hat, that was just a normal night at the bar for them. Unsurprisingly, we had our share of situations there, and I quickly became good at seeing the signs and not being at the epicenter when things happened.

The bar's owner, a guy named Pat, was always ready to go and never scared to get his hands dirty. I'll always remember the night he was throwing a guy out, and the guy must have grabbed every single thing in the bar as Pat dragged him toward the door! Pat would barely pry the guy's hands off of one thing before he'd grab something else — chairs, tables, coat racks, pictures on the wall. The clean-up afterward took longer than it did to throw the guy out!

One time our whole crew got into it with some locals who were being rowdy, and of course Pat came out from behind the bar and got involved. We got this group of guys pushed out into the alley beside the bar, and it was five or six of them against roughly the same number of us, coming together in a "mini-Braveheart" kind of clash. (laughs) As usual, I made sure not to get caught in the middle of it. The Irish guys really liked to fight anyway, so I left them to throw all the punches, kicks and knees. I just stayed on the outer edge of the skirmish and played "goalie" — whenever somebody got pushed out of the action, I'd run around and knock 'em back into play. (laughs) If I remember correctly, it didn't go well for those locals that night.

Crazy Cab Ride

A while later another American guy got hired on, a guy named Bernard, and one night he was talking to this guy who was being drunk and dumb and kicking the sign outside the bar. I wasn't too concerned because it looked like Bernard had things fairly under control, but the guy eventually kicked the sign one time too many. All of a sudden, Bernard snatched this guy up, slapped on a rear-

Me and Aaron after his submission victory at the first-ever bodogFIGHT event in Costa Rica.

naked [choke] and lifted the guy right off the ground! Really chokin' him hard, trying to put him to sleep.

After the guy finally passed out, the weirdest thing happened. Bernard let him go and the guy slumped to the ground, but then he immediately popped right back up and took off running! He reached the street outside the club just as a taxi drove by, and without even hesitating, this guy jumped up onto the hood of the car!

The taxi driver started freaking out and swerving all over the road, with the drunk guy clinging on and yelling, *"YOU SAW THAT! HE ASSAULTED ME! YOU SAW IT!"* It was like something out of a movie, with the guy lying across the windshield and screaming. Of course the cab driver couldn't see anything, and he ended up swerving up onto the curb and taking out a trash can!

That was Seattle, man — it was just this weird, off-the-wall kind of place where even the fights weren't normal, and almost always involved something crazy happening.

Chapter Nineteen

RICK RAVANELLO

All photos courtesy Rick Ravanello.

"*The guy goes right over the fuckin' rail, and I'm fighting to keep him from plunging down a story and a half!*"

Leading-man looks are something that Canadian-born actor Rick Ravanello has always had in large supply, and they've helped him to forge a career that includes appearances in over 100 movies and hit TV series such as *CSI, Weeds, NCIS,* and *Criminal Minds.* But he's not just a pretty face, as he also brings considerable acting chops, extensive gridiron experience, years of Muay Thai training, and a tae kwon do black belt to the table.

As great a guy as he is, I will never forgive Rick for losing a fight to me in the TV movie *Secret Liason,* which snapped an over ten-year-long defeated streak during which I never won a fair onscreen fight.

Damn you, Ravanello. I was proud of that.

Rough Customers

I started bouncing when I was eighteen in Nova Scotia, on the east coast of Canada. I'm kinda proud to have come from that area because it was nothing but crazed motherfuckers. That's all I knew growing up. I was a big kid, five-ten and about 225 pounds, so it was kind of natural for me to work the door. In Nova Scotia clubs, you got almost nothing but fishermen and ironworkers with the occasional coal miner thrown in, so you can imagine the kind of [bouncing] crews that they needed at these places.

The first pub that I worked in was in Lewisburg, at a place called Daniel's. I'd work the taps during the day, then a band would come in at night and I'd stand at the door. There was never any cover charge for those gigs, but being the asshole that I was, I was charging everybody two bucks a head to get in! (laughs) I wasn't making too many friends, but I was making stupid jack at the door.

One night, these guys came in who had been out on the boats for weeks. Crews like that always had all this cash, and they would just sit in the bar and spend and drink. They'd be so sloshed by the end of the night that you usually didn't have to do anything more than gently ask them to leave. But this particular crew, they had tempers, dude. Late in the night, a big fight broke out at one of the tables and one of the guys got kicked in the head. So we dragged him out with him cussin' the whole way, then went back in and waded into his group of buddies to throw them all out as well. Unfortunately, that's not where the situation ended.

At the end of the night I went out to my car, which was a bright yellow 1980 280ZX. It was the only car that looked like that for miles, so everybody knew it was mine. I get in and head home, but I hadn't even gone two miles when the car started shaking all over. So I pulled over, got out, and saw that those fishermen had taken all the lugnuts off my wheels! (laughs) This was before everybody had cell phones, so I had to sit there in the middle of nowhere, no traffic going in either direction, and wait for someone to happen by and help me out.

I can laugh about it now, but when you think about it, the guys who did that were seriously trying to fuck me up. That was my first experience with learning to be a negotiator and not piss guys off, so they're not looking for a way to get back at you.

Charlie's

I moved on to a place in Sydney [Nova Scotia] called Charlie's, which was a more upscale place that had a dress code. That applied to the bouncers, too — we had to wear dress shirts, clip-on ties and suspenders that buttoned onto our slacks. That outfit became a serious problem one night, when a guy we were throwing out reached back and grabbed me by my suspenders! All I remember is this guy yanking so hard that I was pressed right up against the doorjamb, while two of my buddies were frantically trying to unbutton the suspenders from my pants! My face was plastered on the doorjamb, with the dude outside sitting right back on his haunches and pulling like was in a tug-of-war or something! It

felt like forever before my buddies finally got me unbuttoned and the guy went tumbling out into the parking lot. (laughs)

Rick and I lock horns on the TV movie SECRET LIAISON. At one point his performance got so intense that he legitimately choked himself unconscious. No shit.

Hangin' Out

One of the funniest stories happened in a pub in Sydney called The Crow. It had two levels, and the upper level was kind of a deck that ran around the perimeter of the room, about a story and a half up with a long staircase leading up to it.

We heard this ruckus goin' on, bottles smashing and shit, and we ran up there to find a big fight right where the balcony met the stairs. Two of our guys jumped in and started pulling people apart, and I grabbed onto the nearest troublemaker. Next thing I know, the guy tries to pull away and goes right over the fuckin' rail! I've got a hold of him under the arm, and I'm fighting like hell to keep him from plunging down a story and a half! A couple of our other guys leaned over to help but I still had most of his weight, and I had to hold that guy for what seemed like forever. I'm hangin' my armpits on the rail but I don't have the strength and leverage to pull him back over. They actually had to get a rope and hang it over the side to finally get him back onto the balcony!

Smooth Herman's

After that, I bounced over to another club in Sydney called Smooth Herman's that opened at 3 AM. The place had a raised dance floor, which of course was always filled to capacity when the place got going.

On my very first night, a big ruckus starts — everybody on the dance floor is screamin', all the chicks are screamin', and when I run up there they're all pointing at one guy who's standing on the edge of the dance floor with his back to everybody. I walk over to see what's up, put my hand on his shoulder to turn him around, and then just as he turns to face me I see that he was taking a piss off the side of the dance floor! Which means he's now pissing all over the front of ME! No word of a lie, dude, while he's laughing his ass off, this guy soaks me from the chest all the way down to my boots.

Of course I fucking lose it. I grab him in a headlock and start dragging him toward the front of the club. By the time we get to the door, his pants are down around his ankles and he's left a trail of piss all the way through the place! I guess that was my Smooth Herman's christening. (laughs) To this day, whenever I talk to anybody I knew around that time, they always say, "Do you remember when that guy pissed on you at Smooth Herman's?" (laughs)

When It All Goes Wrong

Smooth Herman's had these big oak doors that people would line up outside, and one night this guy decided to rush the front entrance. I guess he didn't want to wait, and figured he could just run through everybody to get a drink. He smashed his way through a few customers before I stopped him at the threshold, and then he hauled off and just cranked me. Hit me hard enough in the shoulder/chest area to throw me back a little bit.

On reflex, I came back and hit him like a fullback hitting a block, right in the chest. [He was] standing with his back about ten feet from the closed doors, and I drove him all the way back into them. When we hit, he smacked his head on the door and dropped right to the ground, then his eyes rolled back and he started doing the funky chicken.

Of course that brought the cops and an ambulance, and although I thought I was just doing my job, they said I was overzealous and they put the cuffs on and arrested me. That started a big nightmare, because even though I was only in custody overnight, it took me two years to get that [assault charge] expunged. It just hung over my head — every time I got pulled over, a red flag would go up. To be honest, I wouldn't be living [in the USA] right now if that charge still stood.

That's what sucks about the job, you can be trying to do the right thing but you still end up in crazy situations that can affect the rest of your life.

The Blue Moon

After that, I started going to school in Halifax and began working at a bar there called The Blue Moon. The only reason I wanted to work there was because they had free pizza for the bouncers. That was their thing, you could eat free pizza all night long so it was a pretty cushy job.

But still, I gotta say that Halifax was a rough town. They don't mess around in that city. One time, I walked the cash to the bank with a couple of guys like I did at the end of every night, and when I came back, you should have seen my truck! They smashed the wind-

Rick looking all cool and tough and manly and handsome and dear God do I hate this guy.

shield, the panels were all smashed, it looked like they took baseball bats and just beat the shit out of it. And I don't even remember doing anything wrong that night! Guys [in that city] would just hate you, dude, even when you didn't know why.

You Never Know

A while back I had an experience on the other end of things — this story even made TMZ — when my buddy [*Dazed and Confused* star] Jason London and I were in a club. Unbeknownst to anyone in our group, Jason got a little mouthy with one of the bouncers. The next thing I know, someone comes running up and says, "Jason's outside and he just got the shit kicked out of him!" I went out and there he was, sitting against the wall with cops all around. I said, "What happened?" and he pulled me close and said, "Dude, they broke my face... and I just shit in my pants!" He was beat up, I mean beat up BAD.

It was all strange to me because I had been fine with the doormen that night. They had even ejected my brother earlier in the night completely without violence, so they seemed like pretty good guys. Even though Jason was shooting his mouth off, it still surprised me how extreme they reacted.

But then I found out that the night before, one of the doormen had had an argument with some guy, threw him out, and followed the guy into the parking lot where the guy stabbed him! That bouncer ended up dying in the hospital two days later. So of course, before Jason even had his incident, the bouncers were already on edge and pissed off.

Now, Jason couldn't have weighed more than a buck-forty and he had two guys [each weighing] over two hundred pounds beating the shit out of him, so that was a little excessive. But at the same time, it goes to show that you never know what a bouncer's already been through, and how hard you're gonna be able to push him before he snaps.

When I walk into a bar, I already know what those [bouncers] gotta do because I've done the job myself. Every night, a bouncer's gotta deal with a bunch of drunk idiots. Everybody thinks they're Superman, everybody thinks they're right, and nobody wants to go home at the end of the night. Bouncers deal with that shit every night, and while of course they should learn to temper themselves, I always stay conscious of what a bouncer might have already been dealing with before I even got there.

🐦 @rickravanello1

📷 @rickravanello

Chapter Twenty

"SUGAR" RAY SEFO

Photo courtesy Ray Sefo.

"I said, 'Look, I'm trying to calm the situation down, so why don't you back off and stop bleeding on me?'"

During its 1990s heyday, Japan's K-1 group ranked as the greatest kickboxing promotion of not just that era, but *any* era. And one of its greatest, most dangerous and charismatic stars was New Zealand native "Sugar" Ray Sefo.

Sefo's innumerable career highlights include a runner-up placing in K-1's ultra-grueling World Grand Prix tournament, and a beyond-brutal 2001 slugfest with future K-1 champion Mark Hunt that contains one of the greatest single rounds in the history of combat sport.

Still training as hard as ever after nearly 90 professional kickboxing, boxing, and MMA fights, Sefo also co-captains the pro MMA team at Xtreme Couture in Las Vegas and serves as the president of the World Series of Fighting organization.

Customhouse

New Year's Eve 1993 stands out very clearly as the nastiest night I ever had as a bouncer. I was running security at a club in Auckland [New Zealand] called Customhouse, and it was a very busy night. I think it must have been a full moon, because we had five or six major brawls that night.

The first one was with a football team. American football, that is — in New Zealand we call it "Gridiron." I got called to the front door after the situation had already started, and there were eight or nine big, monster guys out there. Everybody was well above six foot, the tallest guy must have been six-foot-ten! A buddy of mine named Machlas, who was himself about six-six, was dealing with the issue. The six-ten guy was already bleeding from the nose, so it was obvious that there were punches thrown before I got there.

I stood between the football team and my guys — I think I had six guys working that night in total — and I said to the giant guy, "Listen, let it go. It's obvious that you've already come out second-best, and the more you push, the more people are going to get hurt." But the guy started yelling back at me, "I don't give a fuck about this guy!" and so forth, and while he was yelling, the blood on his face was spraying at me! So I pushed him back and said, "Look, I'm trying to calm the situation down, so why don't you back off and stop bleeding on me?"

I sent Machlas inside in the hope that it would calm the giant guy down, which left me with three bouncers backing me up. Keep in mind, all of the bouncers I had working that night were kickboxing champions. I said, "Look, if I let you go with Machlas you're going to come out second-best again. Leave it alone." Once again he started yelling and spitting blood, and once again I told him, "If you don't stop bleeding on me, I'm going to put you to sleep!" So he leaned close and said, "Is that right?" and *BANG*, I knocked him out cold.

To get to the front entrance you had to climb three steps, then it flattened out, and then three more steps. We were at the top of that staircase when I hit the guy, and he made it all the way down to the bottom. I don't think he was badly hurt but he was definitely snoring. At that point I thought, "Okay, now we have to fight all these big guys," but his buddies just looked at their friend and then said to me, "Listen Ray, we're cool." So, thank God, that one got let go.

But the evening was far from over.

Violent Night

About a half-hour later we had at least 300 people in line out front, with a group of five or six guys at the front of the line. A small guy was with them, like around five-six or five-seven, and I could see straight away that he was so drunk that he could barely stand.

I looked at the guy and said, "There's no way you're going to get into the club, you're too intoxicated." Then I said to his five friends, "I'll tell you what, if you want to take your friend off somewhere and sit him down for an hour or so, get him some water or coffee and sober him up a bit, I can probably let him in after that." But then the little guy looked at me and said, "Well, who the fuck is gonna stop us?" (laughs) And I said, "Well, I guess me and my guys will."

Sefo lays some leather on 4-time world Muay Thai champion Martin Holm
(Photo courtesy Susumu Nagao)

I could see in the little guy's body language that he was about to throw something, and sure enough, without another word he swung at me! I easily saw it coming, and I stepped back and front-kicked him away. And then the fight was ON. That's when we came to find out that the little guy didn't just have five friends, there was more like THIRTY of them! (laughs) It was frickin' RIDICULOUS! Just six of us — eight of us, actually, because two of our barmen were also kickboxers — against this small army.

The police were called, but that fight went on for at least five minutes with not a cop to be seen in sight! It was chaos. One of our barmen came jumping out a front window with two bottles in his hands, and we were all knocking people out left, right and center in the middle of the street. We were basically fighting to defend our lives, and it got to be a really bad street fight. Anything went — people getting bottled, picking up trash cans, it really got out of hand.

Even after it was over, the whole night continued like that. It was crazy! There was a bachelor's party that got out of control, and more. It was probably the worst night of being a bouncer that I've ever been through. Brawls after brawls after brawls, and not just with two or three guys. I think the first group of football players was the smallest [group] with only eight of them, and the rest [of the groups] were anything from fifteen to twenty or more!

Fortunately, everybody [on my bouncing crew] was fine at the end of the night, but I woke up the next day and felt like I just went ten rounds with a professional fighter. During the night, it was so busy and the adrenaline was going so I didn't really think about it, but the next morning I was aching and sore EVERYWHERE.

Monsters at the Door

This story happened during my second year of doing security work, at a two-level club called Candy-O's. It was a great place, one of the best clubs in town, and at one point these two big, BIG monsters came up to the door.

The WWE — or I guess it was WWF back then — was in town at the time, and those guys looked identical to the Powers of Pain tag team. If they weren't The Warlord and The Barbarian then they were two guys who looked just like them, size-wise and everything. They were HUGE.

To get into the club you had to go up an escalator into the front reception, and my buddy Chris was the one they ran ito first. He stopped them because they were dressed as if they had just got done lifting at the gym. He said, "I'm sorry, gentlemen, but you can't get into the club dressed like that." One of them said, "We just wanna go check it out. Who's gonna stop us?" So I stepped forward, pushed Chris out of the way and said, "ME. Now, you've got an attitude and you need to leave right now before I throw you out, right?" I think that at the time I was only 205 pounds or so, and these guys were at least two-eighty or two-ninety. But I was young and dumb and really didn't give a damn. "The bigger they are, the harder they fall" was my mentality. (laughs) They stood there for a second and I could tell that they were thinking, "Either this guy is full of baloney or he's the real deal." Thankfully, they finally decided it wasn't worth it and just said, "Cool," and they left.

After work, I went to a 24-hour club where a lot of the hospitality people would go after the big clubs closed. I had just got there and was standing at the front door talking to a buddy, when five minutes later those same two WWF guys walked up! They saw me and said, "Holy shit, do you frickin' work in every club around here?" (laughs) They were turning around to leave when I told them, "No, guys — it's cool, you can get in here. I don't work here but my friends do, and you can come in." And as they were walking in, the bigger one of the two looked down at me and said, "You know what? You got a lot of balls for a little guy!" (laughs)

Busted

Once I was on my way to visit my younger brother Rony at a place where he did security, and before I got there, he asked this group of six or seven guys who were being rowdy and causing trouble to leave.

When Rony and his crew got the guys outside, one of them turned around and said, "Alright, I'll be back tomorrow night with my cousin. We're gonna come here and whip everybody's ass!" My brother asked, "Who's your cousin?" and the guy said, "He's Ray Sefo, a six-time world kickboxing champion, and he's not gonna be happy with you guys!"

My brother just kept a completely straight face and said, "Okay, you do that — you bring him here and I'll whip his ass!" (laughs) I missed it by only about five minutes, and when I got there the boys were all laughing their butts off. It would have been so great to see that guy's face if I had gotten there in time! Needless to say, they never showed up the next night.

That sort of thing happened several times, but it wasn't always so bad. I remember seven or eight years ago, I was already living here in the US but I had gone home to visit. I was standing at the door of a club with a couple of my friends who were working, and this stranger came up and said, "Excuse me, are you from the US?" I said, "No, I'm from here but I live in the US now. Why?" He said, "Oh, you look just like a really good friend of mine, a world kickboxing champion named Ray Sefo!"

My boys looked at me and I could tell that one of them was going to say something, but I quietly told him, "Just chill." Then I said to the stranger, "Really? Wow, I've heard of the guy but I don't know him. Tell him I said hi!" The guy said that he would and then he walked away, and all my boys were like, "What the hell was that?!" (laughs)

They were kind of pissed off, but to me it wasn't a problem. If it made that guy feel good to say that he knew me, then it was all good with me. That's happened a couple of times to both me and my younger brother, and even to one of my coaches. It's nice and also funny at the same time, to know that I have all these friends walking around who I've never met before in my life. (laughs) It's always great to meet another friend.

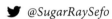 *@SugarRaySefo*

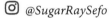 *@SugarRaySefo*

www.wsof.com

Chapter Twenty-One

RYAN ROBBINS

All photos courtesy Brad Carter (TheBradCarter.com).

> *"I see the biggest pair of granny-panties I've ever laid eyes on, unfurling over my head like a parachute!"*

Since his 1997 entry into the film and television industry, Vancouver's Ryan Robbins has become one of Canada's most successful actors. Dividing his time between LA, British Columbia, and a variety of other locations, Robbins has appeared in a number of successful TV and movie productions including *Arrow, Battlestar Galactica, Hell On Wheels, Falling Skies,* and the blockbuster feature film *Warcraft.*

The Littlest Bouncer

In the early 90s I worked at the Royal Theater in Victoria [British Columbia]. I always paired up with a friend of mine, a black dude named Hugo Steele. Swear to God, that's his actual birth name. We did double duty as ushers and security. Now Hugo, you could see him in that job because he was a big, muscular guy. But me, I'm just a little dude, which of course raised a few eyebrows. That's why I had to think of a way to avoid getting physical.

My go-to thing, which I always used to say when someone looked like they wanted to take me on, was to just stay totally calm and say, "That's right, take a good look. Yeah, I'm small. But why do you think I still manage to do this job while being so little?" They'd usually laugh it off, but rarely did they do anything. Just that little grain of doubt in their minds was enough to get me out of a lot of fights.

Tom Jones

Once I was working in the pit at a Tom Jones concert. I was over by the stage stairs because Jones likes to walk down into the crowd and sing directly to the audience, and they needed someone to make sure he didn't get mobbed. I had heard in advance that it was common for him to have underwear thrown at him, so I was expecting that. But I failed to factor in that Tom's fan base had started to get up there in age.

At one point he's crooning to the audience, and suddenly all the light in the place goes dim. I look up to see what's causing it, and there's the biggest pair of granny-panties I've ever laid eyes on, unfurling over my head like a parachute! I have zero time to react before they land right on my freaking face! Man, they were HUGE — if I was claustrophobic, I would have panicked right there. For a moment I can't see anything, just... ugh. After a couple of seconds they slide off onto my shoulder, and as my vision returns the first thing I see is Hugo on the other side of the pit, laughing so hard he's got tears running down his cheeks. I still see Hugo all the time, so not only did I have to go through that traumatic experience, but now I have to get my balls busted for the rest of my natural life!

Cell Phone Carnage

A lot of famous people played at that theater. I met Howie Mandel, and I helped Dennis Miller to locate his wife one night when he couldn't find her. But one of the most memorable incidents didn't involve anybody famous.

It happened during an East Indian rock concert when a fight broke out outside. I ran out the front door and there's this dude with one of those old, brick-style cell phones that he's using like a bludgeon to just beat the pulp out of another guy! Laying that phone into the guy's head over and over and over, just beating the shit out of him. Man, I still remember the sound of it. I run over and help to pull the guy off, and it takes tons of us to do it because he's going nuts, yelling and screaming in some Indian dialect that I don't understand. I'll never forget looking down and seeing that white phone laying on the ground, all busted up and covered with streaks and splatters of blood.

We finally got [the situation] calmed down after the police showed up, and then we learned the reason for the attack. Back in India, the guy who was getting beaten on had been a corrupt cop who imprisoned Brick Phone Guy's brother. In his own language, Brick Phone Guy had been screaming, *"WE'RE NOT IN INDIA NOW!!! WE'RE NOT IN INDIA NOW!!!"* To this day, thinking about that blows me away. I mean, what are the odds of that happening? How crazy is it that two guys with this crazy history in India would just randomly bump into each other at a concert in Victoria, BC?

Nightmare Boss

The boss at that place was a complete asshole. He didn't like me, or Hugo, or Frank, the manager who hired us. He was always trying to find a way to get rid of us, giving us shit details or putting us in compromising positions so we'd either screw up or tell him to fuck off and quit. One night David Duke, a former Grand Dragon of the KKK who was running for President or something, was in town for a speaking engagement and he came to the theater to see a show. His

One for the bossman, one for Mr. Duke.

assigned seat was up in the balcony which was not even in Hugo's section, but the boss said, "Hugo, I'd like you to escort this gentleman to his seat." Of course, Hugo's first response was "NO." But he really needed the job, so he ended up having to take a fucking KKK Grand Wizard to his seat while the boss was just watching him the whole time, waiting for him to fuck up. I have NEVER seen Hugo look so angry, man.

Shortly after that happened, the boss had me, Hugo and Frank arrested on charges of stealing over $100,000 from the theater! The cops showed up right on my doorstep, on Christmas Eve of all days. They gave me the whole, "You can come down voluntarily or come down in handcuffs" routine. So we all spent our Christmas Eve locked in separate holding cells, getting interrogated. The cops tried all that typical movie stuff, "Your friends already gave you up, just confess and make it easier on yourself." Stuff like that.

I was SHITTING myself, praying that they were lying to me, and of course it turned out that they were. So because all of us stuck to the truth, which is that we didn't do shit, they couldn't pin anything on us and they had to eventually let us go.

A month or two later, they finally discovered that it was the asshole boss who had stolen the money, and he was trying to pin it on us the whole time!

🐦 *@RyRobbins*
📷 *@raincityryro*

Chapter Twenty-Two

JONATHAN "THE ROAD WARRIOR" GOULET

Photo courtesy Jonathan Goulet.

"He put a gun to my temple and said, 'I have enough rounds for all of the bouncers here.'"

Identifiable by his garishly-sculpted, multicolored haircuts that at times even displayed a sponsor's name, Canadian mixed martial arts pioneer Jonathan "The Road Warrior" Goulet brought an exceptional level of excitement to the MMA arena during his nine-year career. Out of 35 professional fights he only went to the judges' scorecards three times, and notched no less than four KO victories in 28 seconds or less.

A nine-time UFC veteran and stablemate of UFC legend Georges "Rush" St. Pierre, The Road Warrior helped to carve a path for countless Canadian mixed martial artists to follow.

And it all started with a painful epiphany while working at one of his hometown's "livelier" nightclubs.

Being Shown the Door

This story is the reason I became an ultimate fighter. In 1999, I was working in a club in my hometown of Victoriaville [Quebec]. One night, I kicked a guy out and it went really bad for him. But when I came back into the bar, four bikers who were his friends jumped at me, and it wasn't like in the Jean-Claude Van Damme or Steven Seagal movies. When guys fight you in real life, they don't jump at you one at a time like in the movies. It was four guys, four big guys, and they all punched me at the same time.

I got knocked down and I fell between a metal door and a brick wall. They began opening the door over and over, slamming my head between the door and the wall. They were kicking my whole body, my face — the other bouncers came to help me but it was already too late. By that time, I needed an ambulance.

I managed to get up and walk to the ambulance but I could not walk straight. I felt like I was drunk — I actually laughed and said, "So this is what it's like to be beaten up by four guys!" (laughs)

I knew then that watching Jean-Claude movies and Seagal movies was not enough to teach me to defend myself, so I decided to learn jiu-jitsu and MMA, first at Team Legion and then later with Team Tristar.

Don't Clap When They're Strapped

A few months later at the same club, it was closing time and I was telling everyone it was time to leave. While I was doing that, I clapped my hands very loud. But these biker guys who were standing right in front of me were strapped, and very jumpy, and one guy quickly put his hand into his pants and looked at me very aggressively.

Thankfully, I knew the guy. I called him by his name and talked to him, and he and his friends calmed down. But then another bouncer with bigger hands than mine said, "C'mon guys, let's go!" and clapped again. Then the guy in front of me pulled a gun out of his pants and put it against my temple! He looked at me and said, "I have enough rounds for all of the bouncers here. Now just give me five minutes and I'll finish my beer and leave."

Of course I told him he can have all the time he wants, and he calmed down right away. In fact, he was so calm that when he took the gun away from my head, he showed it to me. I had to admit it was a beautiful gun. (laughs) A couple of minutes later, he finished his beer and told all his friends that it was time to go. After they left, I was standing there thinking "What just happened?" Man, I almost peed in my pants!

A week later it was my birthday, and again I saw that same guy in the club. This time he was jumping at a friend of mine, so I grabbed his neck, choked him out, and threw him out of the club. I was worried that he might come back later, but thank God nobody saw him around after that. In fact, he just disappeared. Maybe he made too much noise in the bikers' world, maybe he died or went to jail. I don't know.

Called on the Carpet

I used to kick out a lot of guys who sold drugs, and sometimes I had to go and have a meeting with their bosses about it. Whenever I had to go to one of their offices, I was always worried about what was going to happen. When I walked into the office, I would right away look around to see if everything was covered with plastic sheets! (laughs)

But they were always very reasonable. I explained that if I could see the dealers selling their stuff in the club, so could any cops who might be there, and the bosses always understood that I was protecting my club and their business at the same time.

After all, better that I ask those [dealers] to leave than have them end up in jail for the night, right?

🐦 *@JonathanGoulet*
📷 *@JonathanGoulet*

Chapter Twenty-Three

GURDARSHAN "ST. LION" MANGAT

All photos courtesy Gary Mangat.

"They put me in the deep freezer — I was shivering and shaking so violently, it was like a seizure!"

British Columbia native Gurdarshan (aka Gary) "St. Lion" Mangat is the first fighter of the Sikh faith to become a Canadian featherweight MMA champion. After rising to prominence as a member of K-1 and Shooto veteran Kultar Gill's MAMBA MMA team, Mangat moved across Canada to join the world-renowned Team Tristar, and train with names like "Ragin" Kajan Johnson, Rory "Red King" MacDonald, and multi-time UFC champion Georges "Rush" St-Pierre.

After accomplishing a major life goal of competing — and winning — a professional MMA bout in India, Mangat has set his sights on becoming the first Sikh fighter to throw down in the UFC Octagon.

Mistaken Identity

In January 2011 I was working at a place called Shark Club in Richmond, BC. I always worked inside [the club] because I was by far the smallest bouncer there. All the other guys were big football players and things like that. I got the job because of my MMA credentials, and also because my size and my ability to get along with almost anyone made me non-threatening, and effective in getting people out without violence.

The crowd we got in that place was mostly Indian guys, and so was our bouncing crew, so there was usually some history between our bouncers and guys who came into the club. That meant trouble, and so did the fact that some of our guys had gotten to like the power of their job, and might have been starting to press it too much with the customers.

One night, just two weeks before I was scheduled to fight for the Canadian [MMA] title, the Shark Club manager put me on the front door because he had just canned the guys who usually worked there for always getting into fights.

It was a UFC night so it got packed quick, and soon the line-up out front was pretty long. Still, I saw no signs of trouble, and I didn't think much of it when, at around eleven o'clock, an Indian guy stepped out of the line and casually walked to the front. A lot of people did that to ask how long the wait was going to be, and sure

L. Gary adds a few more percentage points to his 76% career stoppage record. R. Gary compares six-packs with UFC flyweight champion Demetrious "Mighty Mouse" Johnson.

enough that's what this guy did. But the question was barely out of his mouth when he suddenly pulled out a can of bear mace, and sprayed it directly into my eyes and mouth!

That stuff is really strong, and the spray caught a lot of people at the front of the line as well. Within a few seconds, we were all suffering pretty bad. My first reaction was to run after the guy, but I only [made it] a few steps before the stuff kicked in and made my eyes swell up and my lungs shut down. Soon, I was totally blind and could barely breathe.

I felt my way back into the coat check area just inside the door, then collapsed to the floor and pretty much passed out. By this point, the bear mace had drifted through to the dance floor all the way at the other side of the club. People were literally puking, so they had to shut the entire club down. While all of that was going on I had to stay by myself in the coat check, because the space was so confined that anyone who came in to help me would be affected.

Gary with legendary UFC champ Georges "Rush" St. Pierre (center) and many-time world BJJ and MMA champion Bibiano "Flash" Fernandes.

The fire department eventually showed up, and a couple of firefighters led me to the back kitchen where they stripped me down to my underwear because the bear mace was in my clothes. I was still completely blind and had no idea what was going on. Then they put me in the deep freezer and told me that it was because the cold would keep my pores shut, and keep too much of the mace from getting into my system. Now I was not only in pain, but also freezing. It was BRUTAL. I was shivering and shaking so violently, it was like a seizure. My body didn't know what was going on — I was heated up on the inside from the mace, but absolutely freezing on the outside, and I still couldn't see or get hardly any air in my lungs.

Then the firefighters did the stupidest thing possible and started spraying me down with water. You're not supposed to do that with bear spray, it's actually one of the worst things you can do. You're supposed to use milk, but they obviously didn't know that and so my skin, eyes and mouth just kept burning. They eventually told me that there was nothing more they could do, and that I just had to wait it out. It took about three hours before I finally got to the point where I could see and breathe again. Just BRUTAL.

My problems didn't end that night because when you get maced, some of it collects in your system and it stays there even after the effects go away. So the next day I went to the gym, and when I got on the treadmill and started sweating, the mace all started coming out. Suddenly I was burning and leaking [mace] into the air around me all over again!

A few days later we finally figured out that one of the fired doormen had pissed somebody off, and that person sent someone to retaliate. They must have just told him "Get the brown guy at the front door," and with me fitting that description, I got the retaliation. It's the only thing that makes sense, because I never had any trouble with anybody in that place. I never gave anybody a reason to come after me.

The attack really messed with my head. I was really paranoid after that, to the point that I didn't trust groups of Indian people being around me anymore. Any time I was in a place with a heavy Indian population I'd get really nervous, wondering if I was gonna have the same type of thing happen again. I even kept the security camera footage of the attack on my phone, and kept watching it over and over as a way to force myself to get over it.

Eventually I more or less did, and in spite of what happened I walked into the cage two weeks later and went five hard rounds to win the Canadian featherweight title. While it wasn't a good thing for all that to happen, it's reassuring for me to look back and realize that I didn't let [the attack] get in the way of my goals.

I know now that if bear spray couldn't stop me, then nothing that happens to me in the cage ever will.

🐦 *@saintlion*

📷 *@saintlion*

🌐 *www.saintlionmma.com*

Chapter Twenty-Four

COLIN DAYNES

Photo courtesy Colin Daynes.

> *"This was the type of place where diplomacy was viewed as weakness, so I responded with a nuclear palm strike to the chin."*

Colin Daynes' resume reads like a laundry list of accolades: ten provincial wrestling championships, five national championships, and three first-place finishes at the Canadian Olympic Team trials. And topping the list is Daynes' competition at the 1996 Atlanta summer Olympics as the youngest member of the Canadian Greco-Roman wrestling team.

Since retiring from wrestling Daynes has earned a brown belt in Brazilian jiu-jitsu under world BJJ and mixed martial arts champion Bibiano "Flash" Fernandes, and amassed a number of jiu-jitsu tournament titles along with a 4-1 professional MMA record.

He's also a genetic freak who eats whatever the hell he wants and walks around with a ripped superhero physique, proving once and for all that life is absolutely not fair.

Colin puts a few frequent-flyer miles on his opponent's account.
(Photo courtesy Colin Daynes)

The Million Dollar Saloon

In 2000, I worked as a bouncer at a strip club in Windsor, Ontario called The Million Dollar Saloon. It was well-known for having huge bachelor parties come in from Detroit. The bouncing staff were required to wear tuxedo shirts and bow ties — to be classy, of course (laughs) — but on Saturdays you had to bring at least two shirts because the first one was almost sure to get blood on it.

The guys I worked with were all massive, two-forty and up. One dude was seven feet, one inch tall. He had to duck to get through doors, and at the end of the night when we rearranged the furniture for the cleaners, he would just lift those couches right over his head.

[When I took the job] my wrestling career had just ended and I'd started doing some MMA. I was training with Dangerous Dave Beneteau, who fought in the UFC when they were still in single digits. He even made it all the way to the finals of an eight-man tournament at UFC 5.

MAULER'S NOTE: Beneteau's use of rapid-fire, machine-gun punches while atop grounded opponents made him a pioneer of the "Ground & Pound" style that would later be popularized by UFC Hall-of-Famer Mark "The Hammer" Coleman

So one night this guy was causing problems in Pervert's Row, right at the stage. When I kindly asked the gentleman to leave the bar, he responded with a firm and heavily slurred "Fuck you!" Now, this was the kind of place where any attempt at being diplomatic was viewed as a sign of weakness. If somebody disobeyed you and you didn't take it to a high level right away, you'd either get sucker punched right there or else the sharks would be circling for the

He doesn't just look like a warrior from 300, he can fight like one too.
(Photo courtesy ErichSaide.com)

rest of the night. So I responded to this guy with a nuclear palm strike to the chin with the worst of intentions.

Since the guy was already drunk and not expecting it, he went out like a light. I had to drag him through the crowd to the front door, and we were about halfway there when the guy started coming to. At that point, I started getting him to walk beside me so I didn't have to drag him anymore. (laughs)

We were just about at the door when he looked at me all cross-eyed and said, "What happened, man?" I said, "You fell asleep at the bar." He thought about that for a minute, then said, "Sorry about that. Thanks for helping me." (laughs)

I told him "No problem, go get some rest," and that's the last I ever saw of him!

⊙ *@colindaynes*

Chapter Twenty-Five

BRAD LOREE

All photos courtesy Brad Loree.

"We were stashing bats and hammers all over the bar in preparation for a full-scale attack."

A former professional kickboxer and sparring partner of WKA world champion Tony Morelli, Vancouver-based stuntman/actor Brad Loree has been shot, stabbed, blown up, and otherwise mangled in well over a hundred movies and TV shows. A longtime member of the exclusive Stunts Canada organization, Loree boasts an impressive resume that includes the *X-Men* series, *Watchmen, Twilight: New Moon,* and the TV series *Smallville* (in which he stunt-doubled series star Tom Welling).

But his most notorious gig by far came when he co-stunt coordinated *Halloween: Resurrection* while also starring as iconic serial killer Michael Myers.

Blaine BJs

In the early 80s I worked at a place called Smuggler's Cabaret in Surrey [British Columbia], right on the Canada/US border. I was barely twenty-one at the time, and I was so naive that I was actually blown away by the fact that women could roll in with no money and drink for free all night, or that people would come in and drink their faces off on a work night. I grew up in a strict Christian household — Dad wasn't a drinker and Mom was a Jesus freak — so I didn't know about any of that lifestyle. But I sure learned quick! (laughs)

Sometimes when my shift was over, I'd drive over the border to Blaine, Washington to fill up my tank because gas was a lot cheaper there. One night I was doing that at around 3:30 in the morning, and I looked across the island and recognized an American girl I'd seen in the club that night. We got to talking, and I ended up getting her to jump into my car and drive around the back of the gas station to this dark, narrow service road where she promptly gave me some service.

She blew me for quite some time, until I finally thought, "The girl's put in a champion effort, I better bust it off so she's not down there all night." So I promptly let 'er rip, but no sooner was I done than she looked up and chastised me for coming too fast! (laughs) She said she had a black boyfriend whose cock she would suck for literally hours. Now, I like sex but I'm not obsessed with it, I'm not one of those guys who needs to do a marathon. It feels nice, but not so nice that I wanna do it for hours on end. Get in there, put in a decent amount of time, and get the job done, that's what I say.

Another time, a different girl who was also from Blaine took me down to the Marina where her dad had a boat. We went down into the hull of the boat and she started giving me a blowjob, but by that time it was five in the morning and I was tired from a long shift, and drunk. So while she was doing her thing I laid my head back against the hull, and

Dick Warlock, the HALLOWEEN 2 Michael Myers, meets his HALLOWEEN 8 counterpart.

sure enough I conked out and started to snore! (laughs)

It was so loud that the first snore startled me awake, and of course she heard it too! She looked up and said, "Did you just fall *asleep?*" and I tried — badly — to convince her that I had nasal problems! (laughs) Even worse, these little white speeder pills that bar patrons used to give me — I took them maybe twice, but they never did fuck-all for me — fell out of my pocket. A few days later, her dad found them and she had to explain how these drugs got into the hull of the boat! (laughs) Poor girl.

Wrestle Monsters

Smuggler's had a pretty badass crew that included a guy named Bob Molle. Bob was a huge Greco-Roman wrestler who would later become the only person to win an Olympic medal and also play on a

Grey Cup-winning [Canadian Football League] team. If I remember correctly, he even won the Grey Cup twice. Bob was so tough that he had back surgery just three weeks before the 1984 Olympics and still took home a silver medal, losing only to Bruce Baumgartner, the most decorated American wrestler of all time. So in other words, Bob was a MONSTER.

We also had Eric Froelich, a super-athletic former gymnast and pro wrestler, who was in his mid-forties but still tough as hell. And also Nick Kiniski, a son of the pro wrestler Gene "Big Thunder" Kiniski. Nick was a pro wrestler like his dad, but also a member of the same Olympic team as Bob. As a kickboxer I didn't know anything about what these grappler guys did, but I quickly gained a K2 mountain-sized amount of respect on the first night I saw one of them go to work.

It was about a half-hour before closing, and these two young football players came in. One of them was just a GIANT, and he walked in like he owned the place and started drinking shooters and smashing his glasses on the floor. So Eric went over to tell the guy to get out,

Brad has a brief cuddle with Jamie Lee Curtis before going back to trying to murder her.

and the kid just laughed and said, *"Fuck you!"* Eric said something that got the guy to stand up, and that was the kid's undoing. In the blink of an eye, Eric clamped on a front facelock and had the kid down on the ground, screaming for his mother.

Then Eric lifted and dragged him toward the entrance, into this little eight-by-eight-foot foyer that was between two sets of thick wooden doors. By this point, Eric was so angry he was literally frothing at the mouth. He kept yelling at us to leave them alone in that foyer, but we all knew what would happen if we did, so we eventually convinced Eric to let the guy run off with his tail between his legs. After seeing that, I never had any illusions about a good wrestler's ability to hold his own in a street fight.

Welcome to the O.B.

I got to be good friends with a bartender named Paul, who eventually quit Smuggler's when he was offered a doorman position at a strip joint called the Ocean Beach Hotel — we called it The O.B. After Paul left, he'd call me from time to time and urge me to join him there, since it was better money and he said I'd get treated better by the management.

I eventually made the move, but on my very first night some young psycho glassed a bigger guy right behind the ear. The gash in the big guy's head looked like something out of a porno film, and there was blood EVERYWHERE. I'll never forget the look in the psycho's eyes after he did it, they were as cold and emotionless as a shark's. So of course, I was immediately thinking that I made a big mistake in coming here.

There were also two brothers who used to come in, a couple of throwbacks to the old days. Not full-on bikers but definitely skids, real rough-looking characters who called themselves — I swear to God — Butch and Spike. Sure enough, the inevitable night came when they started some shit with Paul. I grabbed one of them, I forget which one, ran him outside through the front doors and booted him down the steps to the sidewalk. By that point, Paul had already finished doing whatever he did the other brother, and he came up behind me, ran down the steps and punted my guy right in the guts! It wasn't any normal kick, either — more like the kind that would score a 60-yard field goal. It ended up rupturing the guy's spleen!

Of course I ended up talking to the cops, and I tried to cover Paul's ass but he still ended up getting charged. I heard that the injured guy healed up eventually, but neither him nor his brother ever came back.

Evil Rick

One of the regular patrons was a native guy named Rick. About six-foot-two, really lanky with super long, black hair. He had a pair of mirrored sunglasses that he always wore inside, long before that became popular with douchebags, and his eyeteeth were just a little bit too long so they looked like vampire fangs.

Rick was a phenomenal, phenomenal artist. He used to sit at the bar with an artist's pad and pencil, and the shit that he drew was so impressive that people would look over his shoulder and immediately ask to buy whatever he was working on. But he'd always say, "Just buy me a couple beers and you can have it." So while he didn't get rich off his work, at least he drank for free every night.

He came from either North or South Dakota, I forget, and he had served in Vietnam with the US Navy Black Berets. Those guys' job was to go into POW camps and extricate American prisoners. One night, Rick calmly showed me a spot under the mastoid bone which he said was the best place to put a blade if you wanted to kill a person silently. He'd done shit like that for two years and then come home, re-enlisted, and gone right back to do it again. I couldn't believe that he'd want to return to a war that had guys shooting themselves in the leg to get out of it, so I asked him one night why he went back.

He told me that that he grew up on a reservation where his uncle ran a child prostitution ring, and that as a young boy he was victimized by the most sick people you can imagine. You can't even dream up the shit that he said was done to him. So of course he grew up with some anger issues, and he said that Vietnam had been great therapy for him. One night I asked him if he'd taken anyone out since he got back, and he said, "Three people — although one of the guys was a drug dealer who a bunch of us were shooting at, so I can't be sure about him. But I like to think that I was the one who got him." (laughs)

Rick used to be the lone bouncer at Gary Taylor's Rock Room, a really popular club in Vancouver during the 70s. He kept a record of every altercation he got into at that place, and it ended up totaling 168 fights! Rick was a really valuable guy to have around because every time I got into a situation, he was always right beside me. I don't think I could have had a better guy backing my play. I really liked that guy and he was always good to me, although I'd be lying if said that he didn't also scare the hell out of me.

They must have had a thing for hiring Vietnam vets at the O.B. because they also had a guy there named Jesse, who was from Oklahoma and also a vet. By the time I started working there he'd already racked up seven assault charges... and he was only a waiter! (laughs) Whenever there was a fight, Jesse would get this happy look on his face as he fucked people up with pool cues or whatever. One night I was talking to someone about a [Vietnam war] movie I'd seen, and I quoted a line from it: "Napalm sticks to kids." Jesse overheard that and practically lost his mind. I can only imagine the stuff that he'd seen and done over there.

Don't Fuck with Bob

Bob Molle eventually followed me to The O.B. and one night we were both on the door when a couple came in. The guy was fucking HAMMERED, so I said, "I'm sorry but you've already had too much to drink, I can't let you in tonight." The guy looked at me for a second, then kind of dropped his head and his arms as if he was resigned to not getting in.

But that turned out to be a dummy move, because out of nowhere he lunged forward and sucker-punched me right in the face! My head snapped to the right, and in the nanosecond that it took me to bring my head back, Bob had already leaped on the guy and pinned him to the ground, screaming, *"IF YOU EVER TOUCH HIM AGAIN, I'LL RIP YOUR HEAD OFF!!!"* I was so angry, I was circling around in search of an open spot to boot the guy or poke him in the eye or something, but Bob was so fucking huge that it was like the guy had completely disappeared! (laughs) To this day, I can't get over how quickly Bob was able to react while being the size that he was. What an animal. Even Nick Kiniski, who would trash most of his training partners, told me that Bob was the one guy he could never get the better of on the mat.

John the Greek

A while later I bounced at Champagne's Cabaret in a place called Whalley, which is the roughest part of the already-rough city of Surrey. Champagne's stood out because it was kind of a higher-end place in an area where every other place was pretty rough. They even had a dress code, which was kind of unheard of in an area where T-shirts and tractor-tread Daytons were the black-tie of the day.

One night I was switching out some kegs in the back, and the bartender yelled to me that my co-worker Scotty was in some trouble by the front door. I looked over and saw Scotty, who was an incredibly tough motherfucker with a shaved head, standing nose-to-nose with a well-known tough guy called John the Greek. Suddenly, Scotty reared back and hit The Greek with one of his famous headbutts, but instead of dropping like everyone else who'd been on the wrong end of Scotty's forehead, The Greek just chuckled and said, *"Fuck you!"* Next thing I know, they're going toe-to-toe and slugging away.

I ran over and grabbed The Greek, but he was so crazy strong that I couldn't even drag him toward the door. I managed to get him bent over — okay, let me rephrase that — I managed to get him into position for me to clamp on a guillotine [choke], and then I held him while Scotty started bouncin' punches off the guy and kickin' him. He was just pounding The Greek's kidneys like he was a heavy bag, but it wasn't even affecting the dude!

One of the rare moments during Halloween 8 when that hand wasn't either holding a knife or scratching Brad's balls.

We finally got him outside and down on the ground where we started really teeing off and booting the guy right in the face. But still he just reared back up, grabbed Scotty, and threw him over the hood of a car! Scotty came back and jumped on The Greek's back while I kept punching and kicking for all I was worth, and we finally got him to back the fuck off and get out of there.

Still, The Greek wasn't beaten yet. He went down the road to a place called The Scottsdale, where he rounded up a bunch of guys who agreed to help him come back the next day and take us all out. He even phoned up our club's manager and called his shot, saying, "I'm coming back tomorrow and I'm bringing my boys, so tell your guys to get ready."

The next night we were stashing bats and hammers and all kinds of other stuff all over the bar, in preparation for a full-scale attack. But unbeknownst to us, The Greek had made the mistake of trying to recruit one last guy, a massive Asian dude named Steve Harris. Steve looked like Oddjob from the James Bond movies — bald, Mongolian-looking, super barrel-chested, shaved head, and he had this wonky eye that made him look even tougher. We all knew Steve as one of the two or three baddest doormen in Surrey — he'd even done a stint in prison which I'm sure wasn't for jaywalking — so we're talking about one tough customer. But Steve was also really good friends with Scotty, so when he found out who The Greek's intended victims were, he said, "Listen, if any shit goes down I'll be on Scotty's side, fuckface!" And that was all it took to ensure that The Greek's crew never showed up that night.

That's when I learned the valuable lesson that who you know, and more importantly who you get along with, can make the difference between leaving work in your car, or in an ambulance or hearse!

Shame and Redemption

One night a big fight broke out, and while I was tusslin' with this guy I felt someone grab me from behind. Then I heard the head doorman Casey yelling, *"OKAY! STOP! STOP!"*, so naturally I figured it was him who was hanging onto me and I quit resisting. But unfortunately the guy who was grabbing me wasn't Casey, it was one of the guys we were fighting, and I quickly got taken down and pinned to the ground.

After it was all over, Casey looked at me and said, "Well, that wasn't very impressive." As the young guy on the crew who had a bit of buzz around him for being a kickboxer, I was really embarrassed. I was bouncing in an area where everyone prided themselves on being a tough guy, and it really bothered me that I might be looked upon as being inferior.

A few nights later I was still smarting from getting handled like that, when the manager pointed out an older dude who he wanted thrown out for bothering a table of young girls. Initially the guy went along with no trouble, but when we were halfway to the door he started resisting. So I gave him the bum's rush out the side door and slammed it shut behind him.

As you do, I went to the front door to warn the guy working there not to let this dude in. But as soon as I walked up, the door guy said, "Finally! I've been dying for a piss!" and fucked off before I could say a word! So now I was stuck on the front door, and sure enough, the older dude came walking up a minute later. Before he even got close, I pointed at him and said, "GO HOME. Come back tomorrow and I'll buy your first beer, but you're not getting back in here tonight." He threw up his hands and said, "No problem, no problem. I just want to talk to that guy behind you before I go." You know, obviously thinking I was dumb enough to fall for a trick that lame.

I turned my head but kept my eyes on him, and sure enough, as soon as he thought I was looking away he leapt at me. I sure as hell didn't want to look like a fool in Casey's eyes for a second time, so I beat the HELL out of that guy. At one point I was setting up to drive him head-first into a parked van, when this Mr. Goody-Two-Shoes fuckin' patron, one of the regulars, came running out and grabbed me, yelling, "BRAD! STOP!" I've never understood people who do that — how the FUCK is it helping me when you make it HARDER for me to defend myself against somebody who's trying to kill me? I bellowed in Mr. Good Samaritan's face to get the fuck out of there, and thankfully he let go. Idiot.

By that point, the goof I threw out was hell-bent on killing me, and he started to wrestle me to the ground. Now, I wasn't a wrestler, I only knew how to punch and kick, so I couldn't figure out how to break this guy's grip. But as Bruce Lee always taught, "Don't resist, go with," so I dropped to a knee and gave this guy two of the hardest uppercuts I've ever thrown, right in the fuckin' boys!

That broke his grip alright, and as he staggered back I gave him the hardest, straightest right hand, right on the fuckin' chin. He dropped down to all fours and I buried my Tony Llama pointed-toe snakeskin cowboy boot right in this cunt's face as hard as I could. THREE TIMES. But that still wasn't enough, so when I noticed that he was down on an elbow with his head a few inches above the curb, I lifted my knee as high as I could and stomped his face into that curb with everything I had. From three or four places in his face, blood started coming out in a steady stream like a faucet! It was literally splashing on the pavement, so bad that it took three five-gallon buckets of water to wash it all away.

I once read a line in a spy novel that said, "When you fight someone, you want to leave him in such a state that the idea of a rematch never enters his head." I guess I did that with this guy because we never saw him at Champagne's again. Needless to say I was redeemed in Casey's eyes, and thankfully so because I would need his help shortly after that.

Trouble with the PoPo

A few nights later, a guy was yelling at me and Bernie the manager about some bullshit or other. He ended up stomping out of there and giving me the shoulder on the way by, which really, REALLY pissed me off. As he walked away, I just stood there seething until Bernie walked up, gave me a look, and said, "Go whack that cunt."

That's all I needed to hear! (laughs) I set off after the guy, but I was so enraged that I didn't notice that the pigs had shown up. One of them saw what was about to go down, and I was later told that he ran up behind me and was about to grab my shoulder but ended up being a step too slow. I called out to the asshole who'd bumped me, and when the guy turned around I faked a low kick to get his hands down, then stroked him with a beautiful power jab — *BWOP!* Dropped the guy — broken nose, the whole bit — and then the pigs grabbed me and dragged me into the [manager's] office.

They formally arrested me in there, but as they were reading me my rights, Casey walked in and said, "Why are you arresting my guy?" The cops made a big deal about how serious my crime was because I'd "left my jurisdiction" when I stepped out onto the sidewalk. They said that even if the guy himself didn't press charges, they were going to make sure that the local authorities did.

But Casey just stroked his chin and said, "Oh, is that right? You're going to arrest my doorman for knocking out some fucking goof, are ya? Okay, but remember a couple of months ago when two of your guys were trying and FAILING to arrest some dude out front, and it was my guys who saved their bacon? Well, next time that happens, you can take on those scumbags yourself. We'll just sit back and enjoy the show." That got me cut loose in a hurry, because those cops knew that if they went after me, not only would they get no support from Champagne's, but not a single doorman in the entire city would lift a finger to help a cop ever again.

In addition to being a tough sonofabitch, Casey definitely knew how to take care of his crew!

How Things Have Changed

While I don't miss the violence of those days, I do miss the fact that most people behaved differently back then. And by "differently," I mean that they usually took responsibility for their actions.

For example, one time Scotty and I had to stop a couple of guys from coming in, and we were standing above them on a short staircase with our feet around the guys' head level. One of the guys started really beaking off and making a lot of threats, and then he started walking up the stairs. So Scotty booted that fucker right in the face. The guy's buddy started freaking out, but the guy himself just got up, dusted himself off, looked at his friend and said, "Don't fucking whine about it, I had it coming. Let's go."

I saw many examples like that where guys would act like absolute drunken goofs, but when it came to taking their licks, they took 'em like men. Sadly, it ain't like that anymore. Now we've got so many pussies walking around who want to start shit, but run crying to their lawyer when there's the slightest retaliation. It's enough to make you sick.

I guess at some point they stopped making actual men, and started producing the watered-down version that we've got today.

---

www.imdb.com/name/nm0520562/?ref_=nm_mv

Chapter Twenty-Six

JAVIER "SHOWTIME" VAZQUEZ

Photo courtesy Susumu Nagao.

"You could tell that he was wondering, 'How the hell did THIS little guy do that to ME?'"

Jiu-jitsu black belt Javier "Showtime" Vazquez is a member-by-marriage of the legendary Gracie jiu-jitsu dynasty (his father-in-law is UFC co-creator Rorion Gracie) as well as an O.G. of the California MMA scene.

After reigning as King of the Cage (KOTC) lightweight champion through much of that group's early-2000s heyday, Vazquez passed through a number of other prominent organizations including Shooto and World Extreme Cagefighting. Along the way, he racked up a 16-5 record that includes wins over UFC champion Jens "Little Evil" Pulver, and Shooto champion Rumina Sato. Vazquez closed out his mixed martial arts career in 2011, entering the UFC Octagon for the first and only time to defeat fellow former KOTC champ Joe "Daddy" Stevenson.

Today, "Showtime" owns and instructs at the successful Javier Vazquez Gracie Jiu-jitsu Academy in Rancho Cucamonga, California.

Don't Tase Me, Bro

In 2003 I was working at a place in Chino called Godfather's, and one night we had a riot outside. People were fighting all over the place. One of the bouncers had a guy down, and he said to me, "Javi, hold this guy for me." So I put my knee on the guy's belly to hold him still, not hurting him or anything, and the guy was struggling a little bit and trying to get up. He started fighting harder, so I told him, "Dude, just chill out," and then I switched to full mount [straddling his chest]. But he only got worse and became a serious problem to control, so I ended up transitioning to an armbar.

Now we're both lying on our backs and I'm jolting him a bit with the armbar to control him, but not enough to break the arm the way I could have. About ten cops finally showed up, and with them around plus the eight other bouncers who had already handed their guys over to the police, I figured that some of those guys could take over and I released the hold. But this guy was still pretty hot at me, and as soon as I let go he rolled over on top of me and held up his fist. So I swept him and armlocked him again.

Now, I weighed about one-fifty-five and the other guy was around the same size, so it shouldn't have been a problem for this big bunch of cops and bouncers to break us up and restrain the dude. But instead of just coming in and pulling us apart, some frickin' idiot cop TASED me! Well, he tased both of us, really. He was aiming at the dude I was fighting, but one of the taser prongs went right into my knee — and of course it had to be the one that I'd had surgery on just a month earlier! This was one of those tasers that are like little fish hooks at the end of a wire, they embed into your flesh. DAMN did it hurt! After the guy I was fighting was finally subdued, I was PISSED. "Why the hell you tasing ME, dude?!"

I ended up going to the hospital, where they cut my pant leg off to reveal this fish-hook hanging out of my knee. The doctor took a close look at it, and I figured he was about to numb the area and extract the hook with surgical equipment. But instead, without any warning he just grabbed it and RIPPED the damn thing out! Now I'm REALLY losing it. "What the hell are you DOING, dude?!" While I'm yelling, a cop who was standing close by started acting like I was the asshole, and that put me over the top. "First of all, you guys TASED me, then this guy just rips the damn hook out of my knee! What the hell?!!"

Hours later, I finally ended up getting dropped off at the club and limping off toward my car with a hole ripped in my knee and one pant leg cut off at the thigh. Not the best way to end a shift! (laughs)

Bad Listener

A while later, another riot happened after a guy ran up on a buddy of mine — a good twenty-five or thirty foot run — and coldcocked him from behind with this big, looping haymaker. Caught my buddy totally unaware, but he just took it and then turned around and laughed. I ran around behind my buddy's attacker and locked one of his arms up, then picked him up off the ground, slammed him down on his shoulder, took his back and choked him out.

I kept the choke on after the guy was out, but loosened it enough so he could breathe. But when he woke up, he started fighting again. I tried to get him to calm down but he wouldn't listen, so I put him out again. Then I let him wake up and told him, "Dude, I've got a full choke sunk in. Don't fight me or I'm gonna put you out." But once again he forced me to choke him! Three or four times I put him out, until finally he woke up crying and begging, "Please don't do that again!"

So I let him go and stood up. Now, I'm five-seven, and when the dude stood up he was WAY taller than me, probably six-one. I hadn't noticed how big he was during the heat of the moment, and of course when you're on the ground it's hard to tell how tall someone is. But now that we were standing, you could tell that the guy was wondering, "How the hell did THIS little guy do that to ME?" (laughs)

That's a good example of why my philosophy was always, "Choke people first, ask questions second," because if you know what you're doing, you can use chokes to keep everybody safe. You can put 'em out, drag 'em out, and in the end they're gonna wake up just fine. If you apply the choke right and you don't hold it for too long, it's the most humane way to handle violent situations where nobody's gonna get hurt, you know?

🐦 *@javiershowtime*

📷 *@javiershowtime*

🌀 *www.graciejiujitsurancho.com*

🌀 *www.strikebasedjiujitsu.com*

Chapter Twenty-Seven

ROBERT MAILLET

All photos courtesy Aleks Paunovic.

"They had guards all over the place with machine guns, and when the fight started, the promoter called in those guards!"

One of the nicest guys in the world wrapped in one of the most intimidating packages, seven-foot-tall Canadian entertainer Robert Maillet is a prime example of how to make a successful transition from pro wrestling into other forms of show business.

After breaking into the wrestling business in 1989, Maillet wrestled in Canada and Asia before getting his big break with World Wrestling Entertainment (WWE) in 1997. There, he became known and eventually loved as the massive "Kurrgan", and stayed with WWE for a two-year run before returning to the indies.

Not long afterward he retired from the ring to try his hand as an actor, and the combination of his on-camera skills and distinctive look kickstarted a career that boasts such credits as *300, Sherlock Holmes, Pacific Rim, Percy Jackson: Sea of Monsters,* and a recurring role as the villainous "Master" in the TV series *The Strain.*

(Normally) Gentle Giant

The first job I had in security was at my high school. You'd see a lot of crazy kids, fights and stuff like that at school dances. I started bouncing after that at bars, first at a very quiet bar in my home-town of Saint-Antoine, just north of Moncton [New Brunswick]. The name of the bar was Nashville North.

There was one incident where a couple, a girl and a guy, were in a booth and they were arguing. The man was becoming very verbally abusive, and then violent, shoving her and stuff like that. All of us on the bouncing staff were either at the front door or on a low balcony that ran around the edge of the club floor, and there was no easy way for any of us to walk around to the front of the booth. So I came up on the balcony behind the guy, and because of my size I was able to reach all the way over the back of the booth, grab him in a full nelson, and drag him backwards over the railing to carry him outside. He didn't make a fuss after that. (laughs)

I always used holds and full nelsons, stuff like that, but not any really offensive tactics because I was there to stop fights, not start them. Plus, just me being there, my size is kind of intimidating, so a lot of the time when I get there [the situation] quiets down. When they see my size, they're kind of like, "Oh, wait a minute." (laughs) They kind of think twice, which is good. It always worked out for me.

I always try to be respectful to them. If they're not [respectful back], then you gotta do something, throw them out of the bar. If they don't listen to you, you gotta do something. But I tried to never used physical force. I always used my [good] nature, you know, just being myself, be nice to people to calm the guys down.

Montreal Screwjob

After I got involved in wrestling and got hired by WWE, I almost had to do something during that whole thing with Bret Hart, the screwjob [at the Survivor Series pay-per-view] in Montreal when Bret was supposed to win the match [against Shawn Michaels] but the ref and Vince McMahon turned on him. And I was there that evening.

Me and my buddy, Bull Buchanan, we knew what happened and we wanted to leave there [after the match] because we knew that the shit was gonna fly. (laughs) We decided to get out of the building, but the agent — I think it was Gerald Brisco — told us to stay in the locker room. He was afraid that Bret, who was obviously pissed off and upset, was gonna fight with Shawn Michaels. Those guys had altercations before, they never really got along at all, so [the agent] told us to stay so if something happens, we can physically separate them.

But we didn't wanna do that because Bret really helped us get in the company, you know? He was really influential for us, and a friend. We didn't wanna physically step in between him [and Michaels], so we were in an awkward position. But it never really

Maillet with actor Aleks Paunovic.

happened. Bret got in an altercation, but [first] he told us to leave. Vince McMahon came in after that, and apparently Bret punched out Vince McMahon. But we weren't there for that.

Beirut Brawl

Another altercation was in Beirut. We had a [wrestling] tour for a week there with an independent company. There was a mixture of Canadian and American wrestlers there, and the first match was two Lebanese wrestlers, local wrestlers. Something happened during their match that caused an altercation in the dressing room.

Now, this is Beirut, Lebanon, so they had soldiers, armed soldiers, all over the place. It was an uncomfortable thing, them standing there with their machine guns and M16s, looking at everybody. (laughs) And when the fight started in the locker room, the promoter called in some of those guards!

I was stretching before my match, and all of a sudden I see two armed guards running down the steps toward the dressing room! And I'm thinking, "Jesus, there's gonna be a bloodbath. I'm gonna hear some gunshots." But of course, when those [soldiers] showed up with their guns, the wrestlers, they calmed down. (laughs) That was pretty extreme!

Dealing with Mobs

There was one stupid thing that I did at a cottage party in Moncton, in the woods. I was doing security for a little bit of cash, and there was this native guy who was fighting with another guy, whose buddies all started ganging up. The native guy was all bloodied up, they even threw him in the water so he was all wet. But when I stepped in [to protect him], he wanted to fight me! Now I was surrounded by people, they all circled around and they wanted me to beat up [the native guy]. It was an awkward position. I didn't want to beat him up, I didn't want to fight him. Thankfully, it never came to that.

You never know what's going to happen at parties like that, or street fights. Especially when there's a large group of people, you could start a riot. I almost started a riot at a [wrestling] show in India. The crowd was about twenty, thirty thousand people, and the police were holding them back with these sticks. The crowd was crazy. I was wrestling The Barbarian from the Powers of Pain in WWF. We went outside the ring, and in the heat of the moment I grabbed one of the sticks that the police were using and started using it on The Barbarian. But the people got into it too much, and I almost started a riot! The people were trying to climb over the barriers, and the police were beating them back with their sticks! It was pretty wild.

Another time on the same tour we were in this arena, this outdoor cricket stadium, and we were in a tent where our dressing room was. It was about three feet off the ground, elevated. There was this guy, just a small man, who was part of the promotion, helping us, and the guards mistook him as a fan. Two guards grabbed him, and they literally threw him out of the entrance to fall three feet to the ground! I wasn't used to seeing those things, especially in WWE where everyone is professional.

🐦 @Robert_Maillet

Chapter Twenty-Eight

MIKE DOPUD

All photos courtesy Mike Dopud.

"My adrenaline's going and I don't feel anything, so I pull the knife out of my arm and chuck it at 'im!"

Serbian-Canadian actor Mike Dopud has lived nearly as many fantasy lives as the fabled Walter Mitty, with the difference being that Dopud has lived them in the real world.

Prior to his show business career, Dopud jumped back-and-forth between football and hockey, playing for Southern Illinois University, the Canadian Football League's Saskatchewan Roughriders, the World League of American Football's Birmingham Fire, and NHL feeder teams in the East Coast Hockey League and the Quebec Major

Junior Hockey League.

Simultaneous careers as an actor and stuntman followed, until Dopud retired from stunts in 2014 to put 100% of his focus on acting. Since then he has gone from one prominent role to another in productions like *Mistresses, Grimm, X-Men: Days of Future Past, Halo 4: Forward Unto Dawn,* and the Dolph Lundgren/Tony Jaa action film *Skin Trade.*

Add in the fact that he speaks fluent English, French and Serbian, and you have an obvious front-runner for the next time a certain brewery is looking for a new "Most Interesting Man in the World."

Ostatite žedan moji, drugovi.

Merry Christmas, Bumbaclot

I'm working at this nightclub in Montreal around 1992, place was called Xchristopher's. It was around Christmastime, one of those nights when it gets busier than normal. We were already understaffed when my buddy Shawn called in, said his car wouldn't start or something, and that put us even further behind.

The manager of that place — let's call him Jimmy — he was a young guy, around my age at the time, and he was always talking about what a good scrapper he was because he supposedly trained with the Hiltons.

> *MAULER'S NOTE: The Hiltons are a notorious family of Canadian boxers, known as much for their outside-the-ring craziness as for their inside-the-ring accomplishments*

The Hiltons used to come in the bar all the time and just get hammered. They were an out-of-control family, tough as nails, but we knew them so they were cool. They wouldn't pick fights with anyone, they would just try to make us stay until six in the morning and you'd have to kick 'em out.

So Jimmy tells me that since Shawn can't make it on time, or maybe at all, he's gonna have my back. We'd take turns, one guy working the front door while the other guy walked around inside. It worked fine for a little while, but then these three young Jamaican guys come up to the front door. They're already pretty hammered, and I remember kicking them out the week before for getting too rowdy. So I say, "You know, you gotta give it some time. You can come back, but not tonight. Come back next week and I'll buy you all a beer."

Well, the lead guy starts beakin' off, yelling "bumbaclot" and all sorts of Jamaican banter, telling me he's gonna shoot me and cut up me and my family. Now I'm thinking that maybe I'm not gonna let these guys in next week, either. (laughs) So just say, "That's it, you're done," and I close the door.

They start throwing snowballs at the front door and kicking it, and eventually they crack the glass. Jimmy comes walking up and says, "What the fuck's going on?" and I tell him that we should just call the cops, but he says, "I'm gonna go and take care of it." At that moment, one of the bar's employees who was coming to work late opens the door, and the three Jamaican guys bum-rush into the club behind him.

I immediately elbow the first guy and I get lucky, it's a good shot and he goes down. I grab the second guy and put him up against the wall — they were all smaller guys so it was pretty easy — and I have him in a chokehold and I'm choking him out. But while I'm choking him he's holding onto my arms and won't let go, at which point the third guy pulls out a blade and comes at me with it!

Now, my saving grace in this situation was NOT my fucking manager, the guy who said that he was a tough guy and trained with the Hiltons, because when Jimmy saw that fuckin' knife, he just froze. No, what saved me was that the guy with the blade yelled "BUMBACLOT!!!" which got me to turn around in time to see him. But unfortunately I'm still choking his buddy, which is tying up one of my arms so I can't turn around fast enough to get out of the way.

The blade goes across my chest, cuts right through my whole jacket and into my arm, and the point of it lodges in my forearm just below the elbow. Now everything feels like it's going in slow motion, and the kid who stabbed me is all wide-eyed like he's just realizing what he's done. You never know how you're going to react in a situation like that, like, are you going to freak out or whatever. But what happened to me kind of foreshadowed my acting career, because instead of allowing myself to lose it, I just looked down at the knife, looked up at the guy, and said, "Oh, you're a fuckin' tough guy, huh? You have a knife!" (laughs)

My adrenaline's really goin' so I don't feel anything, and I just pull the knife out of my arm and chuck it at 'im! Just missed his head, thank God. Then he picks up a beer bottle, so I grab one too and say, "Okay, now we're even! C'mon, tough guy!" I'm just saying all this stuff that's straight out of the movies. I look back at it now and think, "What the *fuck* are you saying?" (laughs) "Who ARE you?" Finally, he rushes me and I hit 'im with an elbow. I think I broke his cheekbone... actually, I *know* I broke his cheekbone, but I'll get to how I know that in a second.

He drops, and my manager — who's supposed be helping me instead of letting me get stabbed — is just standing there, staring,

Dopud (aka General Black) inspecting the troops in HALO 4: FORWARD UNTO DAWN

white as a ghost. The stabber's two buddies are getting back up and they're freaking out, until one of them pulls a piece.

Oh, fuck.

Thank God one of the bar patrons comes running up at that moment and starts swingin' a pool cue around, keeping everybody at bay. Then the owner comes out and yells that the cops are on the way, so the Jamaican dudes decide to take off. They grab the knife — which I shouldn't have thrown away, because it was obviously evidence — and they're runnin' away, threatening me and shooting their fuckin' guns in the air the way some of those Jamaican guys like to do.

The cops showed up shortly after, and one of 'em points out that my jacket sleeve has just filled up with blood. I hadn't even noticed that blood was first dripping, then pouring out of my sleeve. I peeled off my jacket and saw that the blade had gone a lot deeper than I thought. Just missed hitting a vein, really deep, with the skin all peeled back so you could see the exposed flesh underneath. I ended up having to have surgery because I lost some feeling in my hand.

The cops captured the guys pretty quickly, since all the local hospitals were on alert for three young Jamaicans with bashed faces. They brought them in, and after I got sewn up I went to look at a police lineup and see if I could pick them out. I immediately noticed that the lineup only had four people in it: those three Jamaican dudes and an eighty-year-old man! (laughs) I looked at the cop and said, "Are you fuckin' kidding me? Who do YOU think it is?" The cop just laughs and goes, "I know, but it's a slow night and we couldn't find any other black guys to put in the lineup!" (laughs) Anyway, that's how I knew that I broke the guy's cheekbone, because I saw that his face was all crushed and swollen where I'd elbowed him.

Later on we go to court, and those guys actually try to press charges on ME for aggravated assault and stuff! Those three little punks are in nice suits now, not wearing their gang-banger gear anymore, looking all sad and sorry. And I just lose it on them, "Look at you guys! You're not so tough now, look at you!" Which didn't help my case much. (laughs)

At the end of it all, the judge went easy on them because they were "a product of their environment", uneducated and living in the projects and all that. Then he said to ME that I should have known better and not been so aggressive! I just told him, "Hey, if somebody threatened your life and stabbed you, what would YOU do?" The cops even testified that I was acting purely in self defense, but I still got probation. The Jamaican guys also got probation, plus a restraining order that I didn't think was really necessary. After what happened to them, they weren't gonna be coming back.

After that, every time somebody threatened me while I was on the door, I would just work them right there. If somebody's gonna threaten your life and you get the sense that they're even partially serious about it, you've gotta be prepared to really hurt the guy because they could come back. In this case, I think it only got so out of control because they were scared kids trying to play tough guy. But still, look what almost happened.

I've known three guys that got killed working the door, and three others that got hurt really bad. In the end, you just can't take that chance.

A Shooter You Can't Refuse

In so many ways, bouncing in strip clubs was just a fucking a great job, especially in Montreal. People don't normally go to strip clubs to get into fights, they go to strip clubs to see the girls. And in Montreal it was also kind of an unwritten rule that when you go to a strip club, you tip the doorman when he seats you. A couple bucks here, five bucks there, the players give you ten bucks to seat them by the stage or wherever, and it all adds up.

A lot of the clubs in Montreal were run by the mob, or the Hells Angels, or both. They're all involved, which tells you that there's usually some stuff happening [behind the scenes]. Sometimes I'd be watchin' the club while guys from

Mike showing off his new veneers in GRIMM

different MCs or different families would have their meetings, and I'd have to be ready to let them know if the cops started to come in. There'd be guys sitting there with their faces all scarred or burned, some of the toughest lookin' guys I'd seen. Everybody was always a little tense, and I'd look at these guys talking across the table and think, "Holy fuck, if they get into an argument or something goes wrong, this could get really ugly." Because nobody ever asked me to check their guns or anything, so there was always some serious firepower [at the table].

The mob guys were usually like in the Sopranos with the black turtlenecks and the suits, you know, while the Hells Angel guys were a lot more diverse. But everybody, even when they were friendly, had that underlying threat to them. The mob guys would always send me over shooters of grappa, and if I didn't drink, they'd get pissed off. So you obviously become a good drinker! (laughs)

Puckin' Assholes

Sometimes, members of the Montreal Canadiens would come in, and the girls would all swoon over the hockey guys. Because they had money, they'd pull shit like trying to order all the dancers in the club to dance at their table. C'mon, you can't order ALL of 'em! So now you're arguing with them all night, like, "Come on, guys, I know you're the Canadiens but just take it easy. At least leave five girls for the rest of the place instead of [taking] all thirty!" But they'd go, "Oh, fuck you. Here's fifty bucks, don't talk to me that way."

Me, I didn't give a fuck about how famous they were because a dick is a dick. [Canadiens defenseman] Petr Svoboda, I almost dropped him a couple times for shit like that. "Hey, Mr. Doorman. Take it easy, Mr. Doorman. Here's a hundred bucks for your trouble."

And I'd tell him, "I don't want your fucking money, just don't be an asshole. Because if you keep fuckin' beaking off, I will hit you."

I had a bit more of a temper back then. (laughs)

Hogan and Brutus

One night, Hulk Hogan came into the club with some guys. They had called ahead so we set up tables for them, and they came in and sat down, totally cool. That Red Rooster guy, Terry Taylor, he was there. Super nice, too. And Ric Flair, it stunned me how big that guy's hands and head were. Surprising. A couple of wrestling ladies were there, too, but I don't remember their names.

Brutus Beefcake came in first, but he was kind of like an assistant, you know? He came in to make sure that the club was fine and the girls were okay, things like that. He was kind of hovering around Hogan all night, like, "Okay, boss? Okay, boss? It's good over there, boss! Let's go see those girls over there, boss!" Then he'd come over to me and make sure it was all good, then run back to the table again.

Um... there's something a bit wrong with him, right? Is there? I mean, you know when someone talks to you and you're like, "Uh oh, they're not all there"? That's how I felt with him. The whole time I kept thinking, "Is he joking around, or is this guy for real?" (laughs)

Guardian Angels

One night I was just starting at a new club, buzzing people through the front security entrance that was at the top of a twenty-step staircase. I'm sitting by the door, and after a while I see a Hells Angel wearing full colors in there. He's just staring at me, angrily it looks like, and I'm thinking, "Oh my God, did I kick him out of a club or something?" But it was just that he was trying to figure out where he knew me from, and when he finally remembered, it turned out that we went to elementary school together! (laughs)

Later on that night, a guy got hammered and started acting all pissed off. I guess [a dancer] had touched him a little bit and he wanted more. We tried to calm him down but he got all aggressive, "I just spent five hundred bucks tonight, she better suck my cock!" So I'm like, "All right, you're outta here."

But as I go to grab him, the Hells Angel I went to school with walks up with one of his strikers [prospective members] and goes, "No, it's okay, Mike. I got him." I tried to convince the Angel that it was cool, that he could just stay and watch the girls, but he insisted. And then he and his striker proceeded to take the guy out in a slightly more, um, violent fashion than I would have. (laughs) The guy took a nice little roll down the stairs to the street, and when he got to the bottom, they followed him down and taught him a lesson. Needless to say, the guy never came back.

That club ended up being such an easy place to work because I just had to watch the door and take care of the girls. Every time there was a fight, the full-patch guys and their strikers would take care of it. After seeing some of my friends get shot, and after getting stabbed myself, I felt like that was a nice change of pace! (laughs)

@dopudmike

@dopudmike

www.mikedopud.com

Chapter Twenty-Nine

KEN KIRZINGER

Photo courtesy Gillian Armstrong/Stunts Canada.

"When he saw me coming, he reached into his bag and pulled out a great big fuckin' knife!"

Over the course of a career that extends all the way back to 1983's *Superman III*, actor/stuntman/stunt coordinator Ken Kirzinger has run up a long list of TV and movie roles including a Jaffa warrior in *Stargate SG-1*, a mutant hillbilly in *Wrong Turn 2*, a Viking maraud-er in *Pathfinder*, and psychotic trucker Rusty Nail in *Joy Ride 3*.

But even with all that work under his belt, identifying the biggest role of Ken's career is far from difficult. It came in 2003 when he donned the goalie mask of mythical mass-murderer Jason Voorhees for *Freddy vs. Jason.*

Slackers Swarm the Sleven

During the mid-80s I worked for a security company that hired me out to nightclubs, retail stores, and other places. One night they dispatched me and a guy named Dennis to a 7-11 that was having trouble with teenagers running roughshod over the staff. And sure enough, shortly after our shift began, a big gang of kids showed up and started piling through the front door.

Wanting to keep things under control, we stopped them at the door, limiting the number of kids that could come in at one time so it would be easier to keep an eye on them. That turned out to be a good move, because before long we spotted one of the kids slipping a bag of potato chips and a couple of other items into his jacket. So we waited for him to walk outside and then followed him, because once he was out the door he was officially shoplifting.

We grabbed the kid and started bringing him back inside, but to our dismay that triggered a small riot among his mob of friends. There had to be about fifteen of 'em, girls and guys all in their early-to-mid teens, but at that age where some of the guys had already started growing into men and if they hit you, you were gonna feel it.

We kept dragging the thief into the store, pushing and wrestling with the rest of the mob while the clerk was yelling, *"NINE-ONE-ONE!!! NINE-ONE-ONE!!!"* Thankfully, he was also actually *dialing* 911, as opposed to just yelling it on the off chance that it would make a difference. (laughs)

Ken gives crew member Matty Granger the chop because Matty is a massive douche canoe and totally deserves it. (Photo courtesy Matty Granger)

Dennis and I finally fought our way inside and got the front door closed and locked. Then we dragged the thief into a back room where we planned to wait it out until the cops arrived. But the mob outside wasn't ready to give up, and they started grabbing the biggest rocks they could find and firing them right at the windows! It was like being in a fortress that was under siege, and from the sound of it, those windows weren't going to last forever. Eventually, Dennis and I got tired of hiding and hoping that the cops would show up in time, and we just looked at each other and said, "Fuck this!"

We went back out into the store and ran up and down the aisles, grabbing armloads of canned peas, canned corn, anything we could find that was canned. When we both had all we could carry, we went to the front door, took a second to get ready, and then burst out of there "all cans blazing" like Butch Cassidy and The Sundance Kid!

(laughs) Man, we were winging those cans into the mob so hard — I still remember getting this one kid right in the back. From the sound of the impact, I wouldn't be surprised if I chipped a bone in his spine! After a few of them had gotten hit, we started hearing sirens and that finally convinced the mob to scatter and take off. But man, it was a freaking melee for a while! (laughs)

McDeviant's

Easily the most bizarre night I ever had was when I got sent to a McDonald's on Granville Street [in downtown Vancouver]. At the time, that area was a bit seedier than it is now, but it was still close enough to the more respectable part of downtown that you got families walking in there without realizing that this was no ordinary McDonald's.

When I showed up, the manager came right over to me and said, "Keep an eye out." I asked, "For what?" and he gave me a funny look and said, "Everything, you'll see. All kinds of weird stuff happens here."

Not long after that, the mother of a young girl came up to me and said, "Excuse me, but there's a man over there who keeps looking at my daughter and playing with himself." She pointed at a guy who I could see was indeed staring at her daughter, but from where I was standing I couldn't tell if he was doing anything else. So I quietly circled around behind him, and sure enough he had his dick in his hand, hard as a rock. He was so focused on wanking himself off that he didn't even know I was standing right behind him... at least, not until I leaned in close and yelled, *"PUT YOUR FUCKING DICK IN YOUR PANTS AND GET OUTTA HERE!!!"* (laughs)

The guy practically had a heart attack — he jumped right out of his seat and started scrambling to put his shit away. But he was so hard that he couldn't get it all the way back into his pants, and when he yanked his zipper up, he took a chunk right out of his dick! (laughs) The guy had blood on his hand when he left, and as far as I'm concerned it couldn't have happened to a better guy.

But the night was far from over.

Later, the manager came up again and said that he'd seen a sketchy-looking guy go into the bathroom and not come back out. So I went to check it out, thinking that the guy was probably shooting heroin. But when I got to the bathroom and opened the door, I saw that while the guy was indeed in there, instead of shooting smack he was shoving tampons up his ass! His ass was actually bleeding — I guess he was a prostitute or something — and that was apparently his way of dealing with it.

So what would YOU do when confronted with something like that? I know what I did — I said, "Oops, sorry," closed the door, and just turned and walked away. When the manager asked me, "Was he doing drugs?" I said, "Nope!" and prayed that he wouldn't ask for any more details! (laughs)

A few more hours went by, and it had gotten pretty late when an obviously-drunk native guy came in with trouble written all over him. He got his food, sat down, and almost immediately started yelling about something. So I went over to quiet him down, and when he saw me coming he reached into his bag and pulled out a great big fuckin' knife! (laughs) Thankfully he was REALLY drunk, I mean so drunk that he could barely stand, so it wasn't too much trouble to get the knife off of him and throw him out. But at that point I was thinking, "Really?! All that other stuff, and now this?"

248

As soon as that shift was over I called my dispatcher and told him, "FUCK THIS. You are never sending me to that place again!" (laughs)

Chapter Thirty

CT FLETCHER

Photo courtesy FusionBodybuilding.com

"I think crazy makes up for a whole lotta shit, man. There's no reasoning with a crazy motherfucker."

The rise of YouTube resulted in a number of "overnight" celebrities, but you won't find a single one who is more unique, foul-mouthed, inspirational, or deserving of fame than "The Superman from Compton" CT muthafuckin' Fletcher.

After spending the first eighteen years of his life enduring the physical and psychological abuse of his father, CT developed an obsession with lifting weights. During the 90s he made his name as one of the strongest bench pressers on Planet Earth, putting up numbers as high as 650 pounds and accruing three world bench press titles in drug-tested competition. He added to his notoriety with three additional world championships in the strict curl, setting a benchmark of 225 pounds that remained untouched for decades.

But CT's world came crashing down in 2005, when decades of junk food consumption caught up with him and he was rushed into emergency open-heart surgery. He died three times while having an artificial valve implanted into his heart, and after finally pulling through he was told that he would never lift weights again. Never one to listen to nay-sayers, CT willed himself back into the gym and rebuilt his physique into the obsidian rockpile that it is today.

Once back on his feet and under the iron, he began aggressively preaching his ISYMFS (It's Still Yo Muthafuckin' Set) philosophy in a wildly-popular series of YouTube videos, resulting in innumerable messages of thanks from people who used CT's diatribes as inspiration to slay their own personal dragons.

Currently, CT spends his time endorsing the fast-growing Iron Addicts supplement line, traveling the globe to spread the message of ISYMFS, and training those who have the balls to submit to his torturous but highly-effective methods at the notorious Iron Addicts Gym in Signal Hill, California.

Proving In

I think I got into [bouncing] the way most guys get into it. When you're a big weightlifting guy and somewhat intimidating-looking, it's an easy way to make fast cash. So I was trying to look for fast cash, and some friends of mine who were already bouncers told me that there was an opening at the club they were working at. I don't remember the name of the club — now you're askin' a old man to jog his memory (laughs) — but I know it was in Huntington Park. Not Huntington *Beach*, Huntington *Park*. There's a big difference — Huntington Park is more ghetto, Huntington Beach is where a bunch of rich people live.

Most times it was pretty easy work, most people are civil and accommodating. But on weekends, it's a totally different story — people get too much alcohol in their system, get intoxicated, and turn into totally different people. So that normal guy who don't want no trouble turns into a raging fuckin' lunatic on the weekend when he gets too much to drink. Weekends were the time for, you know, gangs, clubs [to have a] night out. They wanted to go to the club and party, so we had a bunch of outside-the-normal-crowd people who during the week would not come.

You would have guys come in in small crews that have a member of the crew who wants to prove his manhood, prove that he was tough enough to be in the crew, and he would have to go in and start something with the bouncers. I had guys who would come and straight-up tell me that their purpose for being there was to start something, just to prove they were worthy or tough enough. Usually they just got in a skirmish, threw a few blows, got tossed out on their ass, and that was it. They were satisfied [because] they made the crew. That was the normal thing.

But there were two incidents that made me decide that this was not worth it, not worth the fifteen bucks an hour that they were paying me, which was good money but it wasn't enough to risk your life for.

Testing Tippy

There was a young man used to come in every weekend whose name was Tippy, they called him Tippy. He was a neighborhood "street

The Superman from Compton meets The Texas Rattlesnake on THE STEVE AUSTIN SHOW UNLEASHED podcast. (Photo courtesy Steve Austin)

legend" type guy, a big dude with one leg a little bit shorter than the other one. I don't know if that had anything to do with his nickname or not.

Tippy felt that he was an unpaid bouncer, he wanted to do our job for us. So any time there was a little skirmish, Tippy would typically be the first one to run in and grab somebody, throw 'em out of the bar. He loved to be the guy, the go-to guy. And one night Tippy intervened and grabbed a guy to try to throw him out, but this time he grabbed the WRONG guy.

Tippy was around six-eight, and the guy he grabbed was around my height, around five-eleven, but he just happened to be the WRONG guy and he did not wanna be escorted out by Tippy or anybody else. So Tippy did his typical bum-rush and pushed the guy outside, but the guy refused, [saying] "You ain't even a bouncer! I ain't leavin'. I'm comin' back in and there ain't a DAMN thing you can do about it!"

The whole club emptied outside to see this, because this was a guy who stood up to TIPPY. Tippy said, "You must be high or drunk. Don't you know who I am? I'm Tippy!" but the guy's response was, "I don't give a fuck WHO you are!" Then Tippy says, "Well, you must have a weapon, a knife or somethin', because otherwise you wouldn't be talkin' like this." So the guy takes his shirt off and says, "I don't have a GODDAMN thing. There's nothin' but ME underneath this shirt, and I ain't goin' NOWHERE."

Now everybody's standin' around, all the bouncers and patrons are standin' around to see what the fuck happens when somebody defies Tippy the Street Legend. But for some oddball reason that nobody could figure out, Tippy made no advance, no move, no NOTHIN' toward this guy! This guy called Tippy's bluff! Nobody had ever seen that happen before so we were kind of fuckin' stunned — Tippy being stunned more than anybody else!

So this guy goes back into the bar and the crowd parts like the Red fuckin' Sea for him. (laughs) He goes into the kitchen of the bar undaunted, unswayed by bouncers or Tippy or anybody, grabs the biggest butcher knife in the fuckin' kitchen, and he comes the fuck back out DETERMINED that he's gonna do some whittlin' on Tippy's ass that day! (laughs)

Everybody's fuckin' astonished! [Before now] Tippy's been throwing people out left and right, and this guy was no bodybuilding-type guy — he was thin, maybe 160 pounds soakin' wet, five-eleven, but standing up to this fuckin' MONSTER. And everybody's trying to figure out WHY, what the fuck does this guy got that's makin' him, you know, so fuckin' invincible and so brave?

Well I'll tell you, what that guy had was a bucketful of BALLS. He was not intimidated WHATSOEVER, he got that fuckin' butcher knife and he was gonna cut Tippy down to size. And every fuckin' body was just fuckin' STUNNED. We saw this legendary Tippy brought down to a mere mortal by one crazy motherfucker who one-upped Tippy in the crazy department! I think crazy makes up for a whole lotta shit, man. There's no REASONING with a crazy motherfucker. You can't NEGOTIATE with a crazy motherfucker.

So the guy comes out with the butcher knife, and... whenever the bouncers [in that club] ran into that ONE GUY, it was always my responsibility. I was always elected as the one to face that ONE GUY who, if nobody else couldn't get 'im, I'm the last resort. I'm the guy who's gotta get the guy who's got everybody else on "Freeze Mode!" (laughs)

Now, I'm gonna tell you the truth — I would not admit it back then because I was young, and it was impossible for me to admit that anybody could rattle me or shake me at all cuz I was just that fuckin' BAD (laughs) — but this guy had me fuckin' nervous. I was nervous about this motherfucker because he had a WILD look about him. He looked like he wouldn't come at you in any conventional manner — like, this motherfucker's gonna be stabbin' in eight different directions at the same fuckin' time! It crossed my goddamned mind a couple times, is it fuckin' worth this fifteen dollars? Am I gonna risk my life for this fifteen dollars and try to get this sumbitch outta here? OR... is this gonna be the night that I punch the fuck out and don't come back no muthafuckin' more? (laughs)

So anyway, I was elected as I said to handle the situation. And even though those thoughts were in my head, I could NOT... it's so stupid, but I could NOT let those people know, could NOT let the other bouncers, the patrons of the bar, Tippy, or anyone know it was going through my fuckin' mind that I could actually die for this fifteen dollars a goddamn hour. And I'm thinking, what the fuck could I possibly do to get this guy outta here without, you know, dying?

First, I tried to appeal [to him], saying, "Hey man, it's not worth it." I tried to talk common sense. But like I said, talking common sense with a crazy motherfucker is a waste of time, just a waste of fuckin' time. But I was also OBNOXIOUSLY strong, just obnoxiously strong, and I knew that if I could get a hand on him ANYWHERE — hopefully without gettin' the motherfucker sliced off — I would be able to snatch him or subdue him, get him down. That was my belief.

At this time I was three hundred and twenty-five pounds at five-foot-eleven, with twenty-four-inch arms and benching WAY over 600 pounds. Everybody and their mom is doin' that now, but back then there was just a few motherfuckers that could actually do that shit, and even less that was doin' it drug-free! There was one other guy who weighed 400 [pounds] named James "Hollywood" Henderson, he was the guy I was chasing. He benched around 705, and I considered him then — and consider him now — to be the strongest bench presser EVER, because he was known for doin' it drug-free. I don't think any other guy ever benched 705 drug-free but him. And he did it raw, drug-free and raw [without using a special supportive shirt]. I did that in the gym, but it don't count in the gym. You gotta put it together on contest day.

Anyway, I got close enough to this crazy motherfucker that I was able to grab the wrist [of the hand] that had the knife in it and just SLING him outdoors. Just like a rag fuckin' doll, knife and fuckin' all, all the way out the front door and into the parkin' lot! Then I closed the fuckin' door and waited for the police to come and get him! (laughs)

All the guys were pattin' me on the back [after it was over], but I'll tell you I was fuckin' nervous, I was shook up!

The Unkillable Man

After this incident, I said "Fuck it, I ain't goin' back no more."

I'm standing all the way across the club when some of the patrons started yellin' at me, *"CT! CT! OVER THERE! OVER THERE!"* Now, there were usually five to six bouncers in total on the floor at all times, because this was quite a large club and we needed that many bouncers on staff. But at this point [I notice that] all the other bouncers are gone, there's nobody [except me] on the floor.

Then I see all the bouncers gathered in this one fuckin' corner, and I hear a whole bunch of loud cussin' and screamin' and shit. All the bouncers are surroundin' this one guy who's maybe only five-six — FIVE-SIX — but all the bouncers are making NO advances toward this guy whatsoever. Nobody's tellin' him to shut up, nobody's sayin' SHIT.

CT with Fusion Bodybuilding co-president Adrian Burke
(Photo courtesy FusionBodybuilding.com)

I was on my way over, and one of the patrons told me a little story about the guy before I got there. [The patron] said, "Do you who that fuckin' guy is?" and I go, "No, I have no idea who that fuckin' guy is." And the patron tells me that the guy was a high-ranking official in some gang, and that a rival gang had chopped off his left foot and most of his left hand. He had ONE fuckin' finger on his fuckin' left hand, maybe two or three on the right, and half a fuckin' leg missin', and still, NOBODY is fuckin' with him.

The patron told me that the reason why nobody fucks with this guy and he's so fuckin' well-respected is that he was chopped up, mutilated, and left for fuckin' DEAD by the opposite gang, and this motherfucker SURVIVED, came back, and ERADICAT-ED everybody that had done that to him! He killed them all fuck-in' DEAD, man! So he's got, like, super-super-super street cred, and NOBODY fucks with this guy.

I guess all the other bouncers had heard this story too, be-cause one of the bouncers was about six-eight — big dude, BIG dude — and this little guy was pokin' the FUCK outta that big dude's chest with his one fuckin' finger! (laughs) He was like, *"I WILL FUCKIN' KILL ALL OF YOU MOTHERFUCKERS! I WILL KILL EVERY LAST ONE OF YOU!"* The patron had told me, "CT, when this guy tells you that he's gonna kill your fuckin' ass, you may as well say your last goodbyes to your mom and your family and shit, cuz you're DEAD. This guy don't just throw out random threats. He tell you he gonna kill your ass, you're fuckin' dead." And [I'm hearing] all this before I go over there, right? (laughs) I'm like, "What the FUCK, man?"

This little fucker has got everybody's assholes locked up, nobody ain't sayin' SHIT. As soon as I get over there, the other bouncers are like, "Get 'im CT! Get 'im!" and I'm like, "All you motherfuckers is not makin' any advance, and you want ME to go over there and remove this guy that has a proven track record as a KILLER. What the FUCK?"

Just like with the butcher knife guy, I get the thought in my head that fifteen dollars an hour is not worth getting killed over. BUT, I got too much stupid, or too much ignorant, or too much whatever to back down. I guess I'm just gonna be mutilated or dead or whatever, cuz I can't back down.

So I went into "Negotiation Mode" again (laughs), and I went to the cashier and got this guy's fuckin' money that he paid for his cover charge to get in here. I'm like, "Hey, man, we want to refund your money. If you'd like a drink, I'll buy you a fuckin' drink at the bar, but you know, you're disruptin' the whole fuckin' club. Nobody else can party, everybody's here just tryin' to have a good time, and if you wouldn't mind... SIR... (laughs) here's your money back." I talked to him calmly, let him know that nobody was gonna try to throw him out or be physical with 'im, just askin' him to let the other patrons enjoy themselves without this shit gettin' outta hand.

And lucky for me, he was a reasonable guy. He said, "You know what? I like you, motherfucker." And I'm like, "Thank goodness!" (laughs) So I put my fuckin' arm around him, walked him over to the bar, bought him a fuckin' drink, whatever the fuck he wanted, and he was a good guy for the rest of the night, he was calm. But he was not thrown out, he was not escorted out, this motherfucker stayed until he got ready to leave! (laughs)

After that, I don't think I even went back to resign. I just fuckin' said, "You know what? I ain't comin' back here no fuckin' more." I mighta called 'em, maybe called 'em or else I just didn't show up any more. But I already had a full-time job, I'm just tryin' to pick up some extra money on the side, and it was not worth it.

Fuck this bouncin' shit, it's just not worth it.

@CTFletcherISYMF

@c.t.ali.fletcher

www.CTFletcher.com

www.IronAddictsBrand.com

Chapter Thirty-One

CHRIS JERICHO

Photo courtesy Mike McFly and Chris Jericho.

"I'm looking at this twelve-inch screwdriver and thinking, 'That totally could have killed me!'"

If ever a person deserved to be called a "success machine," it would be pro wrestler, actor, author, TV personality, and rockstar Chris Jericho.

After getting his wrestling start in 1990 at Calgary's Hart Brothers Pro Wrestling Camp (where a year later, he'd have the immense honor of assisting with the training of Yours Truly), Jericho quickly parlayed his look, athleticism, and off-the-charts charisma into stardom in the rings of Mexico and Japan.

His major-league career in North America began with a brief stint in Extreme Championship Wrestling (ECW) and a longer run in Ted Turner's World Championship Wrestling (WCW), after which he jumped to World Wrestling Entertainment (WWE) to make one of the most anticipated debuts in company history. Since then, Jericho has accrued almost-innumerable career accolades, including his unprecedented unification of the WCW and WWE titles by pinning "Stone Cold" Steve Austin and Dwayne "The Rock" Johnson on the same night.

Jericho's numerous outside-of-wrestling endeavors include film and TV projects such as *Dancing With The Stars, MacGruber,* and *Sharknado 3,* several New York Times bestselling autobiographies, the enormously-successful *Talk is Jericho* podcast (joined by a growing list of other titles on Podcast One's "Jericho Network"), and a seemingly-endless worldwide touring schedule with his rock band FOZZY.

And to think that all that multi-media success started with a crummy, minimum-wage job in one of Calgary's greasiest dive bars.

Psycho(delic) Circus

At the beginning of my wrestling career I was living in Calgary, and I started working at a bar there called Malarkey's. That was actually where Lance [Storm] worked, too. It was almost like the movie *Roadhouse* [because] there were a lot of bikers in the place, it had that kind of vibe.

Shortly after I started, they began something called "Psychedelic Thursday", which was a weird name for a night where they just played classic rock. Well, it was 1990 so what they played wasn't even classic yet. Their version of psychedelic was your standard Foreigner, Styx,

Journey, that kind of stuff. Basically [they were using the theme] to try to reduce the element of mean guys, and attract more chicks to the club. And while we still got bikers coming into the place, to an extent it worked.

Lance and I got hired because we were almost always available, since we had a lot of time off between wrestling gigs. It was a good job for us because the guy who ran the place was a huge wrestling fan and he totally got it, so he would give us time off whenever we did have a show. Everybody there had a nickname. There was Creampuff, there was Hammer, there was Grizz, and Lance's nickname was Lance Romance because I don't think anybody ever saw him talk to a single chick! (laughs) I was called Biff because with my tan and long blond hair, I looked like a California beach guy.

Generally, it was a really good crew of guys. When you're a bouncer, you're a part of a team — at least you should be — and none of the guys on the Malarkey's team were hotheads. We all wanted people to have a good time, and we did everything we could to prevent fights instead of causing them. I mean, it's not like we were getting paid

A bloody Jericho brandishes championship gold with his Calgary compadres Lenny "Dr. Luther" Olson (left) and Bret "Black Dragon" Como (Photo courtesy Lenny Olson)

enough to get in fights with these idiots. Occasionally a couple of gronks would start fighting with each other and the bouncers would have to jump in, and then maybe one of our guys breaks his hand or gets his nose broken, and fuck THAT, you know?

I wasn't doing anything to hinder the other guys on the crew, but most of the time I would just watch and try to solve things in a non-violent way. That's what I liked about our crew, everybody seemed to think like that. If we ended up with any jerkoffs on the staff, they were gone very quickly because a bad bouncer can add to the problem, and we didn't need anyone making things worse.

Cold Gin

When I first started at Malarkey's, all I ever drank was vodka and orange juice. When I was a kid, I used to listen to the KISS ALIVE album over and over. Before the song "Cold Gin," Paul Stanley does this rap where he says, "I'm sure you people want some vodka and orange juice!" I thought it sounded so cool that I decided it was gonna be my drink, and when I got to Malarkey's I trained everybody to call a Vodka-OJ a "Paul Stanley." Whenever Biff wanted a drink, I would say, "Gimme a Paul Stanley" and they would bring it for me. After a while I started drinking other stuff too, and decided to expand it to where a rum and coke was a "Gene Simmons," and a whiskey and coke was an "Ace Frehley." There was nothing for Peter Criss though, because nobody cares about him anyways! (laughs)

Magic Touch

One night at closing time, a bunch of the biker regulars didn't want to leave. Our guys were trying to get them to go but they kept refusing, and you could tell it was getting to the point where there was going to be some kind of issue, some kind of fight.

So I went to the biggest of the bikers, he was probably around 300 pounds, and I said, "If I beat you in an arm wrestling match, will you go?" And he said, "Absolutely! You're too scrawny, you're never gonna beat me." So I decided to up the ante and said, "In that case, if you lose then you also gotta buy me a bottle of vodka." He said, "Whatever, we'll leave and I'll buy you TWO bottles. But you're not gonna beat me." So everybody gathered around like a prison gang or something, all clapping hands and stuff like that, and we locked up.

Now, at this point I should mention that I wasn't really going into this situation without an ace up my sleeve. A while before, I had been setting up the ring for a show that had [elite arm wrestler] Scott Norton wrestling on it, and we got to talking. He showed me an arm wrestling trick that always works, where if you cock your fist a certain way before you start, it gives you additional leverage and lets you use your shoulder and lat instead of just your wrist. A lot of arm wrestling matches don't show who's stronger, they just show whose wrist is stronger, but if you cock your wrist properly, you kind of eliminate the weak link and bring the bigger muscle groups in. If you do it right, you never lose. I used that trick while I was wrestling in Mexico — went to a bar where there was an arm wrestling contest and beat everyone, became the champion of Monterrey.

So I sat down with this big guy, cocked my wrist, 1-2-3-GO, and *BAM*, I beat him in like, three seconds! To the guy's credit, he got his crew, paid for two bottles at the bar, walked out the door, and that was the last time we saw him. I guess he was embarrassed about losing to skinny me, and he never wanted to show his face again! (laughs)

You Wanted the Best (But Got Me Instead)

I was probably the worst bouncer because I never really wanted to fight anybody. I thought [fighting] was kind of stupid, and I tried to get duties that kept me away from it. At first, I was in charge of monitoring the crowd. The [capacity] was about three hundred and I had to make sure that it didn't get over that. You'd count customers with your clicker at the door, but people would sneak in the back door and throw off the numbers so you had to do walk-through counts as well. Of course, it didn't help that we always had tons of hot chicks [coming around] and I would be letting them in as well. The fact is, I was just bad at that job. We'd have three hundred people in the place and my clicker would read seventy-five, or seventy-five inside and I'd have counted three hundred. So, it wasn't long before they took me off that.

Then they moved me inside, and I would just stand at the back by the DJ booth, playing drums on myself. My chest was the bass drum and my stomach was the snare drum, and I'd just play along with the songs while making sure that everything was cool. If anything did go down and I absolutely had to, I'd get involved, but that usually fell to guys like Lance and some of the others because they were way more organized. To be honest, I was really just there for the girls. That's why I became a bouncer in the first place, to make easy money and hang out with the chicks.

Take It Off (and Wipe It Up)

At one point, Malarkey's decided to have a male stripper night. I didn't know much about male strippers at the time, but I sure was about to find out.

As part of my rounds I had to go into the guys' bathroom and make sure everything was okay in there, and that was also where the strippers were changing. One time I went in there and saw blood on the floor under one of the stall doors. So I knocked and said, "Is everything okay?" and this really shaky voice responded, "I'm fine... I'm fine..." in a way that you knew he really wasn't.

So I opened the door, and there was one of the strippers with a rubber band wrapped around the base of his dick, I guess so he could keep a semi, and he was holding a syringe in his hand with blood all over his cock! I guess he was taking something to make his dick hard — remember that this was pre-Viagra — and he must have hit the wrong vein while injecting his cat tranquilizers or whatever it was. You talk about "draining the main vein," this guy actually did it! (laughs)

The worst part was that the manager said I had get the mop bucket and clean up the male stripper cock blood off the bathroom floor. Probably the worst moment of my entire bouncing career! (laughs)

Hotter Than Hell (at Theo Fleury)

Malarkey's used to use that tactic of keeping a line at the door at all times so that even if the place wasn't full, people would see the line, think it's hot, and want to come and hang out.

One time it was February and really cold outside, and we were holding a line as usual. One guy in the lineup just kept barking and barking about how we were not letting people in. That night it actually was pretty busy — Theoren Fleury from the Calgary Flames was even there — but this guy still had an issue with the line. I was in a bad mood already, and now I had this guy getting on my nerves for a really long time. He finally decided to shove me so I punched him in the face and dropped him, and that kicked off a huge brawl that spilled into the club.

Eventually the cops came, and when they got around to questioning me I knew that I had to cover for throwing the first punch. So with my manager standing right there, I told the cops, "That guy threatened to kill my boss, and NOBODY threatens to kill my boss!" My boss looked at me and said, "Really?" and I said, "Yeah, he totally threatened to kill you!" So then I had my boss on my side, standing up for me, and that would end up being the only reason I didn't go to jail. But for the time being, the cops put me in handcuffs and took me to a back room to wait until they figured out what happened.

So I was back there with my hands cuffed behind my back and who comes into the room but Fleury, who I think was a friend of the guy I punched. If you ever saw Fleury in the NHL you know he was always such a little shit-disturber, and that obviously applied off the rink too because he was gloating and chirping at me like, "Hey Jericho, nice move!" After everything I had already been through, it was the last straw. I started yelling and chasing him around the room, trying to kick him. "Fleury, you fucking asshole! C'mere! When I get these cuffs off..." I'm running around the back room trying to do karate kicks — and I am NOT a karate kicker — and he's just laughing at me through this big gap where his teeth used to be, "C'mon, Jericho, kick me!"

I never did catch the little bastard.

All Hell's Breakin' Loose

Once there was a big fight with this Vietnamese gang that came in, and they were all gathered around in a circle, surrounding me and a couple of the other bouncers. It SUCKED. There was no way to keep from getting hit [because] every time I faced off with one guy, someone hit me from behind.

I ended up taking one guy in a headlock, and then I felt a pain in my chest. I looked down to see blood, and realized that I'd just been stabbed with a 12-inch screwdriver! Luckily, the guy didn't get too deep, he just kind of sliced the skin a little bit. Just after that the cops showed up, and they took the guy down so that his body was pinned down but his head was still free.

At that point I was furious, and I yelled to the cop closest to me, "That guy just stabbed me with a screwdriver!" The cop looked at him, looked at me with the blood on my shirt, and said with a straight face, "I'm not here right now."

So I ran over and gave the Vietnamese guy the NICEST football kick to the face, I definitely felt something crunch when my foot connected. He went to the hospital and six or nine months later, something like that, I had to go to court and testify against the guy. They brought out the evidence in a Ziploc bag, and I'm just looking at this twelve-inch screwdriver and thinking, "That totally could have killed me!"

Nothing ended up happening to the guy because you're supposed to be guilty beyond a reasonable doubt, and nine months after the fight I'm supposed to pick this guy out when all of those guys were the same height, with the same hair... I just couldn't say for sure that it was the guy. At that point I didn't even care anyway. I didn't die and I got my licks in, so whatever.

That's always the thing when you're a bouncer — if you get involved in these skirmishes, the back end of it is such a waste of time. I'd rather just hang out in the back and talk to chicks.

I Finally Found My Way

I didn't end up bouncing for very long. I was pretty lucky in getting [wrestling] gigs, and by '92 I was pretty much wrestling full-time. [My bouncing career] was enough of a taste to satisfy my curiosity about it. When I look back, I see mainly great times — make a couple bucks, hang out, meet some cool people, and if you're lucky there's a girl or two involved, too. If you're gonna hang out in a club anyway, you may as well work there and come home with more money instead of less, right?

@IAmJericho
@chrisjerichofozzy
www.chris-jericho.com

AUTHOR'S BIOGRAPHY

Photo courtesy MasiPhotography.com

Paul "The Mauler" Lazenby spent over 20 years working as a bouncer/bodyguard while doing a wide variety of other manly shit including: battling world MMA champions in the US and Japan; playing Marcus Fenix in the *Gears of War* video game franchise; competing as a powerlifter/strongman; traveling the world as a pro wrestler; stunt-doubling "Stone Cold" Steve Austin; and simultaneously holding three national titles in Muay Thai kickboxing and MMA.

He is also the author of the first *When We Were Bouncers*, which by the time you read this should be widely recognized as one of the most important literary epics of all time.

Suck it, Tolstoy.

 @MaulerMMA

www.imdb.com/name/nm1342807

ACKNOWLEDGEMENTS

Many thanks go out to the following:

Adam Copeland (even though you're a massive dorkus malorkus)
Aleks Paunovic (even though you're gross and I hate you)
Allie Henze
Andras Schram (AndrasSchram.com)
Bas Rutten
"The Bollywood Boyz" Harv and Gurv Sihra
Bonnie Jean Mah
Brad Carter
CM Punk
Colt Cabana
Curtis Braconnier
David Ford (DavidFordPictures.com)
David Leyes (DavidLeyes.com)
Des Woodruff (KenShamrock.com)
Erich Saide (ErichSaide.com)
Everybody at Animatrik and The Coalition
Gillian Armstrong
Greg Mitchell
Jonathan Tweedale
Joy Montgomery
Karen Lansdale
Kimmy Muthafuckin' Chiang

Kyle Gaulin
Kyle O'Reilly
Laura Marks
Marshall Virtue
Mark Kruskol
Melissa Stubbs
Mike Gunther
Mike "Chooch" Mannarino at Forza Barbell
Mitra Castano
Peter DeLuise
Rey Mysterio
Samoa Joe
Shannon Newton
Steve Austin
Steve Wright Jr. (WrightWayPhotography.com)
Ted Fowler
William Blake Herron
William Regal
and everybody I thanked in Volume 1

Made in the USA
Middletown, DE
08 July 2018